DEFENDING BALTIMORE AGAINST ENEMY ATTACK

DEFENDING
BALTIMORE AGAINST
ENEMY ATTACK

—✦—

A BOYHOOD YEAR DURING WORLD WAR II

CHARLES OSGOOD

HYPERION

New York

To our brother Kenneth, born too late to make this book

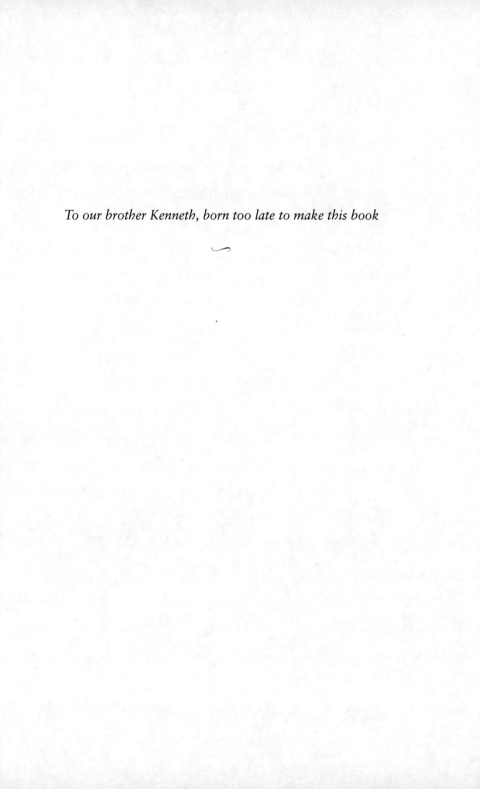

The ball I threw while playing in the park
Has not yet reached the ground.
    —DYLAN THOMAS

CONTENTS

—🍂—

ACKNOWLEDGMENTS

As always, this book would not have been possible without the help of many others, including my sister Mary Ann, whose memory of these events so long ago is sharper and less fogged by time than my own. It was Bill Adler who suggested the book idea, and Will Schwalbe, Mark Chait, Tom Spain, and Ralph Schoenstein who helped coax it into being. My thanks to them and to my own five children, Kathleen, Winston, Anne Elizabeth, Emily, and Jamie, who so often as they were growing up have reminded me of my young self.

DEFENDING
BALTIMORE AGAINST
ENEMY ATTACK

Norman Rockwell's Boy

It was the best of times, it was the worst of times.

Charles Dickens didn't write those words about the year that I was nine in Baltimore, but they happen to fit. That year, 1942, was the best of times for a Baltimore boy who always seemed to be feeling good and the worst of times for a nation reeling from the first blows of World War II. However, in spite of their opposite states, the kid and the country were connected from the moment the year began, a watershed year for America and a long warm bath for me.

On January 2, two weeks before I turned nine, the Japanese took Manila and I sadly had to pin a tiny Japanese flag to the big map I had mounted on my bedroom wall. It would be June 4, the date of America's great victory in the Battle of Midway, before I could happily pin up an American flag.

That wall map of a boy whose name was then Charlie Osgood Wood (I later took as my professional name Charles Osgood) hung above a windup Victrola phonograph, a small rocking chair, and my pictures of Babe Ruth and Franklin D. Roosevelt. Those two men are mentioned in the proper order, because Roosevelt wasn't from Baltimore.

Nine-year-old boys today, to whom a Victrola would mean either nothing or Victrola's Secret, hang pictures of celebrities on their walls; but mine held Great Britain, North Africa, and the Marshall Islands, places I learned about from the front pages of the newspapers that I delivered. I didn't have Kobe Bryant, I had Kobe, Japan.

The Marshalls? Garry and Penny, right? El Alamein? An Israeli rock star, right? Doesn't he have a new single that just passed one by Jakarta? Everyone knows, of course, that Monte Carlo heads a crime family and the Azores are a skin disease.

⌐

Although memory has a built-in sugarcoater, and childhood is seen through the cotton candy of time, I have always been certain that there *was* a genuine sweetness to the days when I was nine years old and the country was united in winning the last good war, if there could have been such a thing. In January of 1942, not only Manila had fallen, but Bataan and Singapore too; London was being bombed nightly; and America had half a navy and an army as strong as Peru's. Things looked hopeless or even worse, but only to those who weren't as mindlessly happy as I was. Not for a moment since December 7 had I expected America to lose the war: I made Donald Duck seem like a pessimist.

And the miracle of that time was that I was hardly a lonely optimist: Millions of Americans were singing "Let's Remember Pearl Harbor" and "When the Caissons Go Rolling Along." And Americans were sustaining their morale with other songs that were calls not to battle but to smile, singing "Don't Sit Under the Apple Tree with Anyone Else but Me," "The Hut Sut Song," and:

You leave the Pennsylvania Station 'bout a quarter to
*   four.*
Read a magazine and then you're in Baltimore.

In that Baltimore, the Orioles flew lower than today's baseball birds because the team was just minor league/international league. There were white wooden houses with big front porches, and grand white stoops that had been famous for a hundred years, and a theater called the Hippodrome that had both films and the nation's last vaudeville shows for twenty-five cents, and the homes of H. L. Mencken and Edgar Allan Poe, and an edifice poetically called the Bromo-Seltzer Tower, the only American monument that involved indigestion. In Manhattan, a college boy met his date under the Biltmore clock; in Baltimore, he met her under the fizz.

And there was milk delivered in bottles and mail delivered twice a day and a boy named Charlie Wood delivering the *Baltimore Sun* and the *Saturday Evening Post*, flinging the *Sun* up to the old white porches like a basketball forward making a perfect feed. I wasn't considered an athlete at nine because no varsity played my sport: the newsprint drive-by on a flying Schwinn.

It was while making those newspaper deliveries, trying to miss the bushes and hit the porch, that I first learned the importance of accuracy in journalism. And while I flew and flung, I used to sing such winged words as

> *Blackstrap molasses and wheat-germ bread*
> *Make you feel so good you wish you were dead.*

I always felt good and wanted to stay alive so I could keep feeling that way, not that death was ever real to me: Every nine-year-old is immortal. And so, I merrily sang about wishing I were dead, never pondering the meaning of those loony lyrics any more than I could translate into English:

Hut-Sut Rawlson on the rillerah
And a brawla, brawla sooit.

I simply knew that I felt in those days happy to be alive and living in a city where a trolley could take me to the Gwynn Oak Amusement Park, one of two amusement parks right in the city. The roller coaster at Gwynn Oak was where I swooped down in my own space shuttle and looked for German saboteurs who might have been trying to sneak into the Baltimore harbor. Of *course* the Germans would want to come to Baltimore, which had more Germanic people than the Sudetenland. None of them, however, yearned for re-union with the Fatherland.

When I was looking down on that city from the top of the coaster's highest hill, I was taking for granted the easy enchantment of an America that was posing for the covers of the *Saturday Evening Post*, an America captured on film by MGM. In fact, many movies about the forties opened with my life: a scene into which a boy on a bike comes riding and tossing newspapers up to porches, where people were learning words like *blitzkrieg, bushido, Vichy,* and *Guadalcanal.*

That boy was often Mickey Rooney, wondering if he could meet Judy Garland at the malt shop to talk about putting on a show. Although evil was on the march all over the world, the America celebrated in the films of 1942 was still an innocent place, where malt had nothing to do with beer and a show didn't need corporate underwriting. It needed only Mickey's and Judy's allowances, an empty barn, and a cast that was paid in milk shakes.

My best boyhood pal was also a girl: my slightly taller, slightly younger sister, Mary Ann, a highly intelligent girl who followed the Orioles and the war—not always in that order—as keenly as I did.

"Montgomery just beat Rommel," said Mary Ann one day. Some of our neighbors might have thought she was talking about a high-school football game, but Mary Ann and I knew that North Africa was no longer just scenes of caravans that you looked at while waiting to see the dentist.

In 1942, Barbra Streisand, Paul McCartney, Wayne Newton, and Muhammad Ali were born, and so was something that would be considerably less entertaining: born beneath a football field at the University of Chicago, the atomic bomb, but my family wasn't informed. My father was brilliant at math and could add a column of figures at a glance, but he knew nothing about radiation. If asked, the average American that year might have said that radiation was what came through the pipes in winter. Nevertheless, the American home front *was* crackling with a different kind of power: irrepressible good cheer.

A two-ocean war was creating cosmic darkness, but we

were inspired by the spirit of an Englishwoman named Mrs. Miniver in the wonderful film of that name: She showed us what pluck could be, a word my mother defined for me.

"It means having the courage to keep fighting when it seems you haven't got a chance," she said.

"You mean like the Washington Senators," I said, referring to the team that always had permanent possession of last place in the American League. "You mean their courage to keep showing up at the games."

"Sort of like that," she said. "You know, Charlie, your father says the only causes really worth fighting for are the hopeless ones."

"So the war is hopeless?" I said.

"Certainly *not*. America never lost a war and we're not going to start now."

How could I argue with a stand-in for Mrs. Miniver?

My Irish relatives weren't crazy about being inspired by somebody English, but they made an exception for Mrs. Miniver because Germany and Japan were the enemies now. Moreover, in spite of having an Irish mother, Mom had a weakness for the English. When she corrected our table manners, she would often say, "What if the queen came to dinner?"

To my great relief, the queen never came. Neither did Duke Ellington.

At the start of 1942, a black heavyweight champion named Joe Louis showed us it was possible to deliver a knockout with a left. A city on the cusp of the South, Baltimore was still segregated in 1942, but that hideous condition didn't stop a boy of nine from seeing in Joe Louis a hero as great as Jack Armstrong, Dick Tracy, and Franklin D. Roosevelt. Some Baltimore fight fans would have said that Louis was brought to mind by the title of one of the year's big songs, "That Old Black Magic." This particular magician, however, could not have gone swimming at a public pool or played softball at a place ironically called Liberty Heights.

In 1942, I was unaware that a gallon of gas cost fifteen cents, and that a loaf of bread cost nine, and I certainly didn't know that the Dow Jones average hit 107. To me, the Dow Jones average would have been what Dow Jones was hitting. *I* wasn't hitting much more than .107 in the sandlot games at Liberty Heights, even though I had prayed for better batting to Our Lady of Lourdes, the namesake of the parish school that was half a mile from my home. To make a good hitter out of someone with *my* hand-eye coordination would have taken a miracle worthy of Lourdes.

What did I look like on most of the days in that ancient year? I can see myself standing by the juniper bushes outside our house, with a brave little tight-lipped smile that seemed to say *Who misses the Bronx?*, where my family had moved from an apartment in 1939. I am wearing a striped polo shirt that never became part of the Ralph Lauren collection, although it might have become a style statement for Ralph Kramden. As a pleasant change from the corduroy knickers that whistled when I walked, I am wearing almost-knee-length wrinkled brown shorts with about two inches of my belt flapping to my left, the fashionable way for belts to flap that year. Attention is drawn away from my brown shoes by three-tone socks, which defy coordination with any clothes known to man. And parted to the right, my dark hair dips down to my left eyebrow, as if I were auditioning for an Our Gang comedy. Like H.L. Mencken, Barry Levinson, and Babe Ruth, I am ready to make my mark on Baltimore, USA.

Because no child has historical perspective, I was unaware at nine years old that the Baltimore of my boyhood was still tied to the nineteenth century by the gaslights on the corners that glowed every evening. I knew the pleasures of watching them flare up as darkness fell over our streets, and of pulling the chains that suddenly snuffed them in the blackouts for air-raid drills. As a passionate part of America's home front, I knew that Hitler would of course make his first target Liberty Heights, a place not far from the fort where Francis Scott Key wrote the song that celebrities are almost able to sing at the beginning of baseball games.

Huddled behind our blackout shades as the sirens wailed

9

across Liberty Heights, I knew that air-raid drills were just a game, because no one had ever attacked the United States, which in 1942 did not contain Hawaii. I hadn't yet learned that the British burned the White House during the War of 1812, or that oil from torpedoed ships had been washing up on the Eastern Shore. I felt safe enough during some of the blackouts to not just huddle but also squeeze: I made lemonade. It was my version of Mrs. Miniver's tea.

10

My family, the Woods

A young woman working in a victory garden

——❦——

Home Front, Sweet Home Front

IN 1942, MCDONALD'S was only a farm in a children's song, but you could get a hamburger at White Castle for a nickel. Your father probably told you it was better to use that nickel to buy another United States War Savings Stamp for your album, which equaled one War Bond: Its $18.75 would be worth $25 in ten years. America needed everything you could give to help fight the Mitsubishis, which weren't elegant cars but enemy planes. I used to dream of flying high over the Pacific and shooting down a Mitsubishi 109 that was headed for one of Admiral Halsey's carriers. I dreamed of being a pilot in the Army Air Corps and being an ace instead of a joker.

On my way to school at Our Lady of Lourdes, I sometimes sang "Comin' in on a Wing and a Prayer" or "Praise the Lord and Pass the Ammunition," for it was all right for American Catholics to bless explosives; in fact, Sister Ursula taught us that St. Barbara was the patron saint of artillery. I also sang a song called "Johnny Zero," about a boy who had missed every question on one school test to earn the name of Johnny Zero; then he had gone into the Army Air Corps, where Johnny the pilot continued to get Zeroes, the enemy's best fighters, and his old nickname took on a glorious new meaning.

As a nine-year-old patriot on the home front, I helped to collect scrap rubber, scrap metal, tinfoil, old newspapers, and even cans of fat for the war effort. Some of the tinfoil came from my father's packs of cigarettes, some of it came from my packs of gum, and some of the rubber came from rubber bands that I took home from school. Stealing them wasn't a sin, because I kept hearing that God was on our side. Praise the Lord and pass the school supplies.

It has been a long time since the army has needed old inner tubes, and no one ever sings when launching a rocket, but the spirit of the American war effort during World War II was so explosive that it even turned city people into home-front farmers, creating what were called victory gardens in our own backyards.

Mary Ann and I happily planted seeds in our victory garden, whose major crop, unfortunately, was pumpkins.

"I hate pumpkins," I told her while we were working in the garden one day. "How will pumpkins help to win the war?"

"I don't know," she said. "Maybe we'll drop them on the Germans and the Japanese."

"Mary Ann, the war isn't a *food fight*."

"I was *joking*."

"Well, I'm not joking about pumpkins. I don't like 'em."

"Charlie, no one cares what you like."

"Well, if anyone asks, it's bananas. Why don't we plant *them?*"

"They grow in Nicaragua," she said. "You ever see a banana tree in Baltimore? They don't even have 'em in the Bronx, and New York has *everything*."

"I wish we could plant *roast beef*."

"Don't you know *anything?*" she replied. "Don't the nuns call you the Professor?"

"Yeah, that's me."

"Well, you don't *plant* roast beef."

"Well, *I* was only joking. Like Charlie McCarthy."

"One Charlie like that is enough."

"But I *am* going to plant something delicious."

"Charlie, nothing delicious *grows* in a victory garden—just vegetables, what people hate."

"I'll find something."

⌐

We had made that victory garden under the direction of our father. Dad made us prepare a backyard plot, about ten by fifteen feet, by digging the soil, removing the grass, weeds, and stones, and raking the plot to plant the seeds for vegetables and flowers that we had gotten at school. It was the first manual labor of my life, labor that must have made me decide on a career in which I would be digging only for words. In addition to the terrible pumpkins, we planted lettuce, carrots, radishes, squash, marigolds, and daisies. How marigolds and daisies would be blows to the enemy I did not understand. Although I was no dummy—at nine, I could already play the piano and the organ, and write bad poetry—the things I did not understand were still an impressive list. And through the years, that list has continued to grow.

16

⌐

"Do the Japs have victory gardens?" I asked my father one Sunday morning in early March while we were preparing the soil to win the war.

"They probably do," he replied.

"Well, it'll be a *losers*' garden," I said, and he laughed, a sound I loved to inspire. "You can't win with rice."

"You don't grow rice in a garden; you need a field," he said. "But the Japanese have always had wonderful tiny gardens. You see, they have very little land."

"So that's why they want America? To make bigger gardens?"

He laughed again. "Not exactly. By the way, did you know that the Japanese even have *rock* gardens?"

For many days after my father had made that revelation, I wondered how the Japanese were able to grow rocks. A formidable foe they would be. But I also had a formidable plan: to grow something we could actually eat.

My own mental weeds were evident when I tried to understand a wartime job that my father took: He kept selling textiles by day, but in 1942 he began working as an expediter for the American Copper Company. Now even prouder of him than I had always been, I mentioned his heroic war work one day to my friend Willard Wallaby.

"My father's really fighting the Germans and Japs now," I said. "He's an expediter."

"An extra fighter?" said Willard.

"No, an *expediter*."

"What's that?"

"I can't tell you."

"It's a military secret?"

"Right."

And that secret was secure because I had no idea what an expediter did, even though my father often did it on the phone in our house.

"Hey, you can tell *me*, Charlie. I won't tell nobody."

"Sorry, Willard. Loose lips sink ships."

"But I don't *know* any Germans or Japs."

"That's what they all say."

⌐

I did understand rockless victory gardens, and our little one was just one of millions in a time when America truly was one nation indivisible, a time when everyone was singing *We did it before and we can do it again*. I didn't know what we had done before besides hold Fort McHenry, but I was certainly ready to do it again; I didn't know why I was growing daisies or why I was collecting newspapers and fat; but I kept watering and collecting while I sang

*There'll be bluebirds over
The White Cliffs of Dover,
Tomorrow, just you wait and see.*

18

"That's one silly song," my friend Ralph said to me one day at school.

"Why's it silly?" I said.

" 'Cause I've been to Dover and it's got no white cliffs, or green ones either," he said.

"You've been to *Dover*?" I said. "You've gone to *England*?"

"*That's* not where it is. It's in *Delaware*. And I didn't see any *bluebirds* either. May as well write a song about Cincinnati."

19

An old-fashioned radio

—🍂—

I'll Be Seeing You

As VIEWERS OF *CBS News Sunday Morning* know, I always end my TV broadcast with words that some people may feel are confusing:

"I'll see you on the radio."

Do these words mean that I will spot you sitting on top of your Bose? No, they mean a great truth that I first discovered when I was nine and spent a large percentage of my life under the spell of American radio. Although I also liked movies, none had ever left me as spellbound as the Theater of the Mind our Crosley set conjured up in the living room of 3504 Edgewood Road.

I feel sorry for kids today, who see a literal Spider-Man on a cinema screen. The kids of my generation, the second or third greatest, would have looked at that guy and seen an actor in a Halloween outfit. The radio, however, sent our fancies soaring beyond what any animator's art could achieve. The sounds of the radio inspired my imagination to create worlds that were both fantastic and as real as the blackout curtains that we closed during air-raid drills. My Superman had three dimensions, possibly four; but put him on a TV or movie screen, where the pictures pale before those on the radio, and Superman is a guy in ballet tights wearing a cape as an unfathomable fashion statement.

The radio of the forties was so powerfully alive that I even knew what the Shadow looked like, and he was *invisible*. Of course, *everyone* in radio was invisible, but we conjured up our own pictures of what they looked like. Imagine: Edgar Bergen became a radio star as a *ventriloquist*! In radio, no one was able to see him move his lips. In radio, he was able to throw his voice across the entire country.

The actor who played the Shadow, Orson Welles, had done another broadcast that made an entire nation think that Martians had landed in New Jersey. Could an alien invasion ever be convincing on TV? No matter how creatively you dressed the aliens, they still would look as though they had come from a planet called Wardrobe.

The horror stories on radio were so believable that I felt

chills as I dove under the covers. The problem was that my radio already was under the covers, where I was supposed to be having sweet dreams, not sponsored nightmares. For my father, "Lights out" meant an air-raid drill; for my mother, "Lights out" meant time for sleep; for me *Lights Out!* was a horizontal visit to hell.

American radio of the 1940s had such a profound influence on me that it is the reason I am doing what I do today instead of selling linoleum or playing the organ at a skating rink. By the time I was nine, I knew that radio was a marvel in which I wanted to spend my life. In what way, I had no idea; but I could imagine no career more delightful, except perhaps to play shortstop for the Orioles. That dream, of course, was unrealistic: I was afraid of ground balls, and few shortstops enter the Hall of Fame with that particular quirk.

23

It had to be radio. Inspired by the legendary voices of Lowell Thomas, Gabriel Heater, Charles Collingwood, Robert Trout, and Edward R. Murrow, I dreamed of broadcasting dramatic news, as the principal of Our Lady of Lourdes had done one day late in the previous year when she had interrupted a Sunday-afternoon performance to tell us, "Children, I'm afraid I have alarming news: Our naval base at Pearl Harbor has been attacked by the Japanese."

"What's Pearl Harbor?" said Willard Wallaby as we ran out of the church.

"I have no idea," I told him. "Maybe a harbor where they do a lot of diving for pearls."

"Why would the Japanese attack pearl divers? I bet they got plenty of their own."

"I guess *every* country can use more pearls."

"Well, the women can. The attack was for *them*?"

My conversations with Willard Wallaby often had the coherence of *It Pays to Be Ignorant*, a program I loved, on which three panelists said funny stupid things. Willard could have been its intern.

⌐

Radio so possessed me when I was nine that I actually looked forward to being sick so I could stay home from school and hear such entertainments as *The Breakfast Club*, a morning show that always concluded by having its listeners march around the breakfast table. While boys my age in Germany and Japan were marching for conquest, I was parading for pancakes.

How rich with radioactivity was that time! However, the only thing that glowed was the fancy of a listener, especially if that fancy was in the head of a child.

⌐

It is late Sunday afternoon and my homework can wait because what's more important: knowing the capital of Bolivia or catching an archcriminal? I didn't know what an archcriminal was. One with good feet? Well, no matter how good his feet were, he couldn't escape from the Shadow . . .

Hear that supercilious cackle? It's Lamont Cranston, wealthy young man about town, cracking himself up by going invisible once more. This vanishing act is more than a party trick: It spells defeat for another archcriminal, until next Sunday at five for Blue Coal.

The Shadow was radio at its best, a bewitching phantom of your imagination. Years ago in the Orient, the pre-PC name for Asia, Lamont Cranston had picked up the power to cloud men's minds. No one knew if he had learned it in a Burmese bordello or a Shanghai school for hypnotists, but he always did it just in time to send the villain crashing into the furniture while spraying bullets at the walls. No villain ever felt dumber than one who shot up the draperies while trying to find the Shadow, who could also have been hated by decent men for that obnoxious snicker.

Cranston was just one of radio's modest private citizens who transformed themselves into invincible lawmen from another world. There was also Clark Kent, a mild-mannered reporter with a personality as badly split as Cranston's. Whenever evil began catching on, Kent ducked into a city room closet, changed to blue tights, red cape, and matching monogrammed jersey, and dropped his voice two octaves:

(TENOR) This is a job for . . .
(BASS) Superman!

While his perpetually bewildered sweetheart, Lois Lane, wondered where he had gone *this* time, Clark Kent was at two thousand feet, daring the enemy to dent his bulletproof chest. He easily could have cheated on Lois because his virility was infinite, his speed was that of sound, and his X-ray eyes could have scouted any bedroom. No one ever asked who covered Kent's beat while he was overtaking bullets, or how he could change both his clothes and voice in three seconds, or why other reporters never found his embarrassing costume in the closet. We believed it all.

Always visible was Jack Armstrong, the pride of Hudson High; he had spent eighteen years there. Jack distributed justice with the help of three sidekicks: Betty, Billy, and Uncle Jim. The first two were teenagers and the third had the mind of one: He seemed to know less than the Lone Ranger's horse. Jack, Billy, and Uncle Jim never laid a hand on Betty; all radio friendships were platonic. And no hormones would have bubbled in a date between Henry Aldrich and Little Orphan Annie or between Corliss Archer and Oogie Pringle. Radio's adolescents reached millions but never reached puberty.

⌒

Superman and *Jack Armstrong* were two of several fifteen-minute adventures, to which Mary Ann and I were addicted, every afternoon between four and six. They were airborne narcotics: If you heard any one installment, you were hooked until the story's last installment, when you had five seconds to turn off the set before the next story began and you were hanging from a cliff once again.

Almost every day after school, I went directly home, looked at my homework assignment, decided not to rush into it, and then heard *Captain Midnight, Dick Tracy, Hop Harrigan, Terry and the Pirates, Mandrake the Magician, Superman, Jack Armstrong,* and *Tennessee Jed*. It wasn't easy to keep track of eight stories at once, to keep Dick Tracy out of Hudson High and Jack Armstrong from making Uncle Jim disappear. By the time I got to Tennessee Jed, I was hanging from seven different cliffs.

Jed was a questionable hero: He began each episode by shooting someone in the back. And he wasn't exactly the fastest gun in the Southeast. In fact, he never saw the target until a bloodthirsty flunky said, "Thar 'e goes, Tinnissee!"

27

Then Jed raised his rifle and shot out the spine of the poor fleeing varmint and the flunky cried, "*Got* 'im, Tinniseee! Daid center!"

We believed it all because, no matter how fantastic, it was still so real: the Shadow making himself disappear and Mandrake erasing everyone else, Captain Midnight and Hop Harrigan landing even when the airport was closed, and Jack Armstrong spending two decades in high school without having been tossed to a tutor. It was all unbelievable, yet it all checked out to the smallest detail—if you didn't count the hormones that never awakened.

28

Radio took infinite pains to preserve verisimilitude; it had a respect for its audience that I have always tried to emulate. I have never wanted my listeners to learn how I cloud their minds.

In 1941, when the actor who had played the Lone Ranger since 1933 was killed by a car in Detroit, the character suddenly came down with laryngitis. To enable listeners to accept a replacement, the Lone Ranger's voice returned slowly, restricted first to just a few whispered words until finally rising to his full, rich "Tonto, go to town and get supplies."

"Me go, Kemo Sabe," said Tonto, a model for the syntax of Cookie Monster. Tonto would have preferred to shop at a 7-Eleven on the prairie because he wasn't popular in town, where he made all of the grubby free spirits uneasy. They saw him as the agent for Mister Self-Righteous.

⌒

When I was nine, my parents sometimes took Mary Ann and me to New York to visit our great-grandmother, Frances Wilson, who was ninety-one and known as "Little Grandma" to us. On one visit, I decided to entertain her by playing something on her Steinway baby grand.

"Little Grandma," I said, "would you rather hear the 'Minuet in G' or the 'Sonata in C'?"

"I'd rather hear *The Lone Ranger*," she said, glancing at the clock and then turning the dial of her big Philco.

"You like *The Lone Ranger*?" I said in astonishment, having thought that her taste ran more to Texaco's *Metropolitan Opera*.

"Doesn't *everyone*?" she said.

The Comanches, Cherokees, Seminoles, Sioux, Apaches, and Navajos certainly didn't.

And so, she had passed up Beethoven and Mozart for Rossini's *William Tell Overture*, the one piece of classical music that every kid in America knew.

⌒

I have a memory of radio's *The Lone Ranger* that is even stranger than my great-grandmother hitting the saddle. *The*

Lone Ranger's first sponsor was Silvercup Bread, for which his horse Silver was named. However, one day the program's sponsor changed to Bond Bread and I think the Lone Ranger's horse then became Bondie. Or was it Treasury Bond? At least I'm sure that his horse never was Arnold.

Did he ever cry "Hi ho, Bondie," words that would have left the bad guys shaking more with laughter than with fear? Probably not: I may have dreamed the whole story but radio *was* like a great dream, so brightly visible while also unseen. One of the popular songs at the time was "I'll Buy That Dream," and I certainly did. No money was needed for it: I simply had to tell my mother to keep buying Ovaltine, Wheaties, and whatever bread was naming the Lone Ranger's horse.

Forties radio had a potent effect on people who were even more important than a nine-year-old Baltimore boy. The program called *Mister District Attorney* always began with a ringing vow by Mister District Attorney, who was in love with the sound of his own voice. In words that I have remembered for sixty years, in spite of my efforts to forget them, he said, "And it shall be my duty as district attorney not only to prosecute to the limit of the law all persons accused of crimes perpetrated in this county, but to defend with equal vigor the rights and privileges of all its citizens."

The impact of radio? There are American cities that have used those words to swear in new district attorneys, even though the language borders on the baroque. It might be better for the new DAs to simply say, "Who knows what evil lurks in the hearts of men?" That would serve notice that they were not inclined to accept a plea bargain.

⌇

In those golden days of radio, I never minded the intrusions of sponsors because many commercials were entertaining. I used to go to school singing "L-A-V-A, L-A-V-A," and "Have you *tried* Wheaties?" and "Don't despair, use your head, save your hair, use Fitch shampoo." A nun who had been trying to teach me math kept me after school one day after I suddenly had been moved to cry, "Call . . . for . . . Philip . . . Morris!" I thought that was uncalled for.

Mary Ann and I used to sing one song that the Communists could have used as an example of the decadence of the capitalist way:

We feed our doggie Thrivo,
He's very much alive-o.
Full of pep and full of vim.
If you want a peppy pup,
You better hurry up
Buy Thrivo for himmmmmmm.

I don't know if that song was the low point of American advertising—it was certainly down there—but I do feel that it may have helped to hasten the coming of public radio. Those songs and slogans were lyrical leeches that fastened themselves to your brain. Your brain had a permanent imprint after just one hearing of

Pepsi-Cola hits the spot,
Twelve full ounces, that's a lot,
Twice as much for a nickel too,
Pepsi-Cola is the drink for you.

"Well, *I* Swan, don't you?" said one announcer in a pitch for a soap that needed a Rosetta stone to find its sense.

Of course, the stupidity of a thought never kept me from expressing it, so that year I found myself saying, "Well, *I* Swan, don't you?" to people who could think of no reply, except perhaps, *Well, at least his* sister *isn't nuts.*

"Charlie," my father said softly after dinner one night, "if you say, 'Well, *I* Swan, don't you?' one more time to me, I'm going to make that soap your dessert."

Radio commercials, whether in English or not, were more than just fun to sing: They also gave us the chance to send away for prizes, such as decoders that could translate secret messages from Captain Midnight, Dick Tracy, and Little Orphan Annie. All of the messages had the same secret: Tune in tomorrow to receive another secret message to keep listening. It was a slightly larcenous loop.

A more useful prize came from the Lone Ranger: For a Cheerios box top, he sent you a magic weather ring that turned purple whenever it rained. Any time you were walking down the street and wanted to know if it was raining, all you had to do was look at your ring.

Yes, my church and school were Our Lady of Lourdes, but my radio was a kind of miracle too, a magnificent world both invisible and as real as the market where I shopped for my mother with ration stamps. Programs like *Inner Sanctum* and *Lights Out!* sent our malleable little minds into realms so terrifying as to make the Wicked Witch of the West seem like the Flying Nun.

A bittersweet example of the innocence that all children had in those radio years was the Halloween when I actually dressed up in a gown as Snow White. I have a feeling that none of the folks I shook down for candy that Halloween thought I was Snow White, just a boy with an ill-advised mother. However, my mother attached no stigma to a son being Snow White; Mary Ann could have been Richard III. Just as anything was possible in radio, the possibilities were also unlimited on Edgewood Road in 1942. I was my mother's prince and her princess too.

One day that year, the nun who taught fourth grade at Our Lady of Lourdes said to our class, "Children, how many different kinds of transportation can you name?"

"Roller coaster!" cried one boy, deciding to skip such insignificant ones as trains, planes, and automobiles.

"Yes, William, that's an excellent answer," said the teacher, showing why she was properly placed in the Sisters of Charity.

"Roller skates!" cried a girl, naming the other major one.

I don't know if anyone named mule train, because my mind, not Mensa-bound, began to drift and dream and again I was hearing the sounds of a world more real than Baltimore, the sounds that linger there still:

Hello, Duffy's Tavern, where de elite meet t' eat . . . Weight: 237 pounds; fortune: danger . . . to be dumb, to be dense, to be ignorant . . . not only to prosecute to the limit of the law all persons accused of crimes perpetrated within this county, but . . . don't despair, use your head, save your hair, use . . . a closing message from Colonel Schwartzkopf . . . Coming, Mother! . . . For eight silver dollars, can that lady tell me . . . how can you *be* so stupid? . . . Good evening, Mr. and Mrs.

North and South America . . . and his wife Belle . . . I'm David Harding . . . I'm a baaad boy! . . . Ah, there's good news tonight . . . No names, please . . . This . . . is London . . . Anaheim, Azusa, and Cucamonga . . . I usta *woik* in that town . . . From out of the night steps . . . Cecil B. DeMille, hoping you will be . . . Good to the last drop . . . Stop the music! . . . This is a job for . . . Leeeroy! . . . and all the ships at sea . . . and that garbage scow brings us back to Miss McConnell . . . Have you *tried* Wheaties? . . . with the mustard on top . . . Last call to breakfast . . . But we didn't even thank him . . . Aren't we devils? . . . Mister, that masked man is . . . Henry Aldrich . . . Likewise, I'm sure.

No one in the class that day named the most powerful transportation of all: radio, which transported us to places that even Steven Spielberg cannot reach.

I remember one particular play by radio's greatest writer, Norman Corwin. *My Client Curley* was about a caterpillar that did a little dance whenever the boy who carried it around played "Yes Sir, That's My Baby" on his harmonica. Aware that the William Morris Agency wasn't overrun by caterpillars with rhythm, the boy was about to use Curley to achieve fame when the worm turned and became a butterfly, one that didn't respond even to "Chopsticks." The poor boy had learned that an agent should represent only non-metamorphic talent.

If that enchanting little fantasy were told on film or tape today, wondrous computerized art would create a Fred Astaire of a caterpillar. However, you would *know* you were watching wondrous computerized art. On the radio, you saw a real caterpillar that knew how to dance, a remarkable talent for a performer who had no feet.

For this Baltimore boy, the greatest show on earth wasn't the circus; it was the show I saw from the fifth row center of the Theater of the Mind. At intermission, I was sold not lemonade but Ovaltine, Wheaties, and Fitch shampoo to save my hair. Much of that hair is gone now, but the sounds of forties radio beneath it will never disappear.

Our white wooden house with a big front porch

Babe Ruth was a New York Yankee, but he was from Baltimore

———🍂———

The Endless Play Date

A MAJOR CAUSE of my boyhood happiness was baseball, which in the forties glowed in a way that has vanished from American life. I will never forget the particular sweetness of being outdoors in twilight in Baltimore, a sweetness known in the days before air-conditioning from Boston to St. Louis, wherever Americans listened to baseball games on radios near open windows. Because all the Baltimore fans were tuned into the same game on WBAL, I was able to stroll down Edgewood Road and follow all the action without missing a pitch.

Yes, in cities from the Atlantic to the Mississippi in that second year of the war, the open windows were speakers.

The alluring night sounds in Baltimore weren't birds but broadcasters talking about a two-footed flock called the Orioles. These broadcasters were describing the world's greatest game in a time when soccer was still restricted to Bolivian picnics and Bulgarian junior highs. The previous year, baseball had reached a new height: Ted Williams had hit .406, Joe DiMaggio had hit safely in fifty-six consecutive games, and I had looked better than ever when I struck out—in fifty-six consecutive games, I believe.

If the weather reports in those days had monitored the air quality, it would have been deemed more than acceptable: It would have been rare. The hills were alive with the sounds of hitting by people like Sherm Lollar, who soon would be going to the Orioles' parent club, the Cleveland Indians, and Felix Mackiewicz, a splendid center fielder who was known as the Polish DiMaggio. To some of us Orioles fans, DiMaggio was the Italian Mackiewicz.

Of course, the Orioles were a minor-league team, like some of the major-league teams today. The Orioles, however, had a wonderful announcer named Bill Dyer. He was what the fans call a "homer," who offered listeners an alternative to professional broadcasting by always rooting for the home team in Memorial Stadium:

"O boy, we sure could use a run now," he would say. "We Birds have *got* to turn this thing around and get at least *one!*"

In rooting on-mike for the Orioles, Dyer struck some people as a man who was for the birds in every way. And if you happened to be for the visiting team, you might wish that an eagle would carry him off. But not me: At the age of nine, always "sticking with them birds," I loved Bill Dyer and wanted his job.

On those summer nights that seem light-years ago, the only way that a strolling boy might have missed a pitch would have been if someone had foolishly turned the radio to *Charlie McCarthy, Baby Snooks,* or *Burns and Allen.* The magic of radio was so strong that we even heard broadcasts of road games, which in those days were faked in a Baltimore studio. Using the Western Union ticker to follow the progress of the game, the studio announcer enriched the quasi-verisimilitude of the action with a device that made the sound of a bat hitting a ball, followed by the recorded roar of a crowd. The ballpark was full of canned fans and it all was done so cleverly that it would have fooled anyone under six.

Not only was there a roar track, but there was even an occasional cry of "Get your peanuts!" and "Ice cream!" and "Beer here!" The broadcasters doing those road games had to be more creative than any of us at CBS radio today, who are simply putting together words; sometimes the Western Union wire broke down, and the man at the mike had to fill the air with fancy rich enough to convince the listening fan that the broadcaster was still following the game and not wallowing in a void.

> Robinson steps out of the box . . . A purposeful little stride . . . Not too bold, not too prissy . . . Using both his legs . . . One after the other . . . Now he bends down and gets some dirt on his hands . . . Five fingers on each one . . . Hands that hit .304 for the Birds last year . . . Guess he also wouldn't mind having some mud from Chesapeake Bay, where the water temperature is now . . . oh, let's call it about sixty-five degrees . . . That's Fahrenheit, of course . . . Now Robinson steps back in again . . . Takes a good look at Maxwell on the mound . . . also known as the rubber . . . and then a quick glance up at a passing Pan Am Constellation . . . Wonder if it's carrying any supplies to our brave allies fighting the war, whose number is Two.

For any boy who loved baseball as much as I did, and there was no such boy, the highlight of the year was the World Series, back in a time before it had become a wintry evening event. For the World Series of 1942, played in the afternoon on grass with no TV, a Baltimore fan who couldn't go to Yankee Stadium or Sportsman's Park in St. Louis could follow the game either on the radio or on a huge simulated

diamond on the wall of the *Baltimore Sun* building downtown in Sun Square.

The radio, of course, was better than watching light-
bulbs on a building, for I could see Stan Musial, Mort
Cooper, Joe Gordon, and Spud Chandler on the diamond in
my mind. Because the nuns at Our Lady of Lourdes were Sisters of Charity, one of them, Sister Ursula, took pity on
small baseball fans and brought a radio to my classroom for
the 1942 Series. Sister Ursula was also a realist: She knew
that none of her students could have been thinking about the
products of Portugal while also thinking about the pitching
of Beazley.

"He who would know the heart and mind of America
had better learn baseball," a distinguished teacher named
Jacques Barzun once wrote. Jacques, how hard I studied that
heart and mind from April till October. I didn't know all the
multiples of nine, but I did know the daily batting averages
of Keller, Moore, Slaughter, Rolfe, Dickey, and DiMaggio.

⌒

Every month of the year, even deep into winter, I bur-
nished my baseball glove, a possession I treasured the way a
boy today treasures his Web site. That *glove* was a precious
Web site, and to make it as professional as a major leaguer's,
I rubbed it endlessly with something called neat's-foot oil,

43

the source of which no boy in America knew. Neat's-foot sounded to me like an Indian chief, but I knew that the Indian game was lacrosse—the Baltimore game too: It was the only city in America where boys played lacrosse in the street.

"I wish you took care of your teeth the way you take care of that glove," said my mother one night. "I don't see you brushing much."

"Mom," I said, "you can make the Orioles with no teeth, but your *glove* has to be in shape."

And caries were *good* in the glove.

I loved that glove so much that I often wore it when I wasn't playing, prepared to catch any random fly ball that might suddenly appear in Liberty Heights; and I gave the glove so much lubrication that a ball might have slid right off it. At night, I put a baseball in its pocket and put the glove under my pillow, the loveliest lump on which to dream.

"You waiting for the Baseball Fairy?" Mary Ann once said. "You want him to take the glove and leave you a ticket to a game?"

⌐

I needed no fairy to see a ballgame, because my father knew the Orioles' manager, Tommy Thomas, and Thomas not only invited us to Memorial Stadium, but also two or

44

three times introduced us to the players, who gave us auto-
graphs that are absolutely worthless today. But what a thrill
it was to get them in the place that in *Bull Durham* is called
"the cathedral of baseball."

There is no high equal to the one of walking into a ballpark and getting your first sight of the field, of pure rich
grass and not the green cement of Astroturf. Taking a trolley
to the park by myself was a kick, of course; but then came
the heady moment of walking into the cathedral. The man
who wrote "I don't care if I never get back" had the wisdom
of Plato. Too bad Plato never had a chance to see the Athens
Athletics play Sparta.

As a traveling salesman, my father was away a lot, selling blankets and sheets and Indian Head cloth; but when he
was home, there was nothing that the two of us liked more
than to go to Memorial Stadium and see the Orioles play,
even though they were a Triple-A team that often played
Double-A ball. In 1942, many players had gone into the
armed forces and the teams played badly. The Orioles, of
course, were capable of playing badly at full strength, if that
expression could have been used for them.

But I never brooded about how often the Orioles missed
the ball, both at bat and in the field, because the important
thing was The Game and I loved it fervently. Today, America's children could never imagine the richness of the plea-

sure I drew from baseball, a wondrously complex game that gives you something in every performance you have never seen before. True, this something was often a new variety of Oriole ineptitude, but the entertainment was still there.

One Sunday at Memorial Stadium, as the guests of Tommy Thomas, my father and I saw an exhibition game between the Orioles and an all-black team called the Baltimore Elite Giants, pronounced *Eee*-lite. To all the closet Confederates in Memorial Stadium that day, the visiting team was seen not as a group of baseball professionals but as Pullman porters out of their league. And out of their league they *were*: They were far better than the Orioles.

"Why aren't those Negroes playing in the major leagues?" I said to my father.

"Well, Charlie, they're flashy, all right," he said, "but they're not steady enough to play the whole season."

My father was a decent and intelligent man, but that observation wasn't one to be bronzed. Like the rest of Baltimore, he never dreamed that his own Babe Ruth might not have been as good as the black Josh Gibson, a catcher who one season hit eighty-four home runs; or that the great Red Ruffing might not have been as good as Satchel Paige, whom a Ruffing teammate named DiMaggio called "the greatest pitcher I ever faced" after trying to hit against him in an army camp game.

My father and I both had a lot to learn. In just four

years, one of our lessons would be a Montreal second base-
man named Jackie Robinson.

⌒

"You know, Babe Ruth came from Baltimore," my father told me at the park one day.

"He *did*?" I said. "Wow, we had the best there ever was.
And now we got a lot of guys that stink. How'd that happen,
Dad?"

"Well, we never *had* Ruth; he was just born here and
then he played in Boston. And as for all the guys that
stink . . . Well, Charlie, you can't love a team only when it
wins."

"You think we'll ever have a chance to try that?"

⌒

Baseball so dominated my days that I also collected
cards of the players that came in bubble-gum packs. Today,
many of these old cards are worth a lot of money. Mothers
who threw them out have said that no one could have
known their eventual value, but that is a weak excuse. A
friend of mine stopped speaking to his mother for several
years because she had thrown out baseball cards that could
have put his son through college.

I used to trade those baseball cards; but had I been able
to sell them, I would have had to give the proceeds to my fa-

47

ther. My parents didn't want Mary Ann and me to have too much money, so he collected whatever I made from mowing lawns, delivering the *Baltimore Sun* and the *Saturday Evening Post*, and selling subscriptions to a Catholic newspaper, and then gave me an allowance. In other words, feeling that money gave us too much freedom, our parents ran a little Communist commune. No matter how much we earned, we turned it over to them and then received an allowance of twenty-five or fifty cents a week. If parents tried this domestic shakedown with a nine-year-old today, they would get a letter from a lawyer.

One time, I redirected my earnings away from my parents and learned that even God took a dim view of child labor. With money earned from selling subscriptions to that Catholic newspaper, I sent away for a prize: a penknife. And when it came, the first thing I cut was myself.

"Charles, you're *bleeding*," said my mother, who didn't miss much. "How did you cut yourself?"

"I think it was with a knife," I said, taking a good guess.

"From the kitchen?"

"From the church. I sent away for it. I'm sure it's okay with Sister Serena."

"I don't care if it's okay with Saint Augustine. You *know* what your father wants you to do with your earnings."

I certainly did: surrender them to loving extortionists.

"And using them to buy a *weapon*," she said. "Well, I'm really surprised."

She was surprised because I had always behaved angelically. I may not have been the best-behaved boy in Baltimore, but I was among the top cherubim.

Perhaps it was her love for Franklin D. Roosevelt that moved my mother to join my father in running their little welfare state. My sister and I considered it unfair; feeling disconnected from our labor, we were deprived of the satisfaction of reward for work we had done. Our parents did, however, have a point: Rather than allow money to burden their children with too many options, they simply paid all our expenses. In American homes today, where the children are in charge, a nine-year-old would give his money to his mother only if she was going to invest it for him, preferably with an insider trader.

49

⌐

It was, of course, a time of much more play than work, and the play almost always was merrily improvised, not organized by adults. Structure? The only structure was that we had to restrict all our play to the city of Baltimore. In that innocent time, a soccer mom would have been a mother who played for Brazil. The lives of forties children weren't organized as if they were wee CEOs: The kids weren't driven in any way, neither pressured to be superkids nor chauffeured from one activity to another by a mother hell-bent on admission to Harvard, perhaps by the time the child was six.

In 1942, the words *free play* weren't shameful because that was, happily, all we did: Every kid made it all up, using only our own resources, and we never had a "play date." A play date was any date that you played. My play dates were 1939 to 1950.

⌒

In a big vacant lot on Copley Road, just a block from my house, I played many pickup games of baseball, in which the first side to bat was decided by two captains moving their hands up a bat until one captain couldn't hold it. There was something about this ritual that revealed the unique appeal of an American boyhood.

In that baseball, where a game boy was any kid with sneakers and a love for the masterpiece of sports, I never once played in a game that had eighteen boys; I didn't even *know* eighteen boys. Creativity is truly tested when you play baseball with five on a side. If one kid is in the middle of the infield, a double play becomes a unique challenge; and if you use someone from the other team to be your catcher, you find that he doesn't have his heart in plays at the plate.

I often played baseball with far fewer than five on a side. I used to love to lie on my back and endlessly toss a ball in the air to myself, counting the number of times I could catch it in a row, never unhappy that I alone was the entire game.

⌒

Every boy of the forties was given the same schedule by his mother: Go out and play and don't get run over. The style of your auto-amusement was up to you. Your mother never drove you to an hour of tossing a ball in the air or carving a stick with a knife or flying a kite or making a slingshot or throwing a football to your dog. She never scheduled an hour of lying on the grass and finding animal shapes in the clouds. She never called another mother to say, "Would Henry like a date with Charles to make stink bombs today?"

Perhaps the most remarkable thing about my boyhood was this: Never once did I say "I'm bored," and never once did I hear any other boy say it. Boredom wasn't invented until 1982.

⌒

In those pre–Toys "R" Us days, we did have digital toys because we made them with our fingers. Using only a wand that I had rubbed with cloth to create static electricity, I was able to fly an airplane made of thin silver foil, a private little airline that to me was the best toy since the invention of the wheel. In fact, the man who had invented the wheel could not have had as much fun with it as I had in my bedroom control tower, directing those silver-foil flights above a runway rimmed by dirty socks. And I also amused myself for hours with wooden blocks, Lincoln Logs, a Tinker Toy, and an Erector Set.

I wonder how a boy today would handle a Tinker Toy.

"These sticks," he might ask. "Are they for Chinese food?"

And an Erector Set?

"What is this?" he might say. "Real reality or virtual?"

"Those are real three-dimensional pieces," his mother would reply. "Would you like to build something?"

"My money market account."

"No, darling, I mean with that Erector Set."

"It's missing batteries. Anyway, I'm bored."

"But you haven't even tried it yet."

"I thought I'd get a head start."

I was also interested in moving money, but not in a portfolio. If you give a nickel to an American boy today, he will want to take it to *Antiques Roadshow,* for he knows that a nickel hasn't bought anything since Herbert Hoover's time. To me, however, a nickel was another toy for my nimble fingers: I loved to set one spinning on a table, to Mary Ann's delight, in the days when spin didn't mean a politician's revision of the truth.

"Spin one, Charlie!" Mary Ann would say and I would begin my merry spin cycle, doing it so well that I could sometimes spin a nickel and two quarters at the same time. The next time a small child tells you that he is bored because he has to kill ten minutes between judo and mandolin lessons, say to him, "Why don't you spin a little change?" Yes, say that and see the judo tried on *you.*

Or ask him to play marbles and he'll think you've lost your own. But marbles was a great American game when I was a boy and I spent hours flipping them around the floor. What were they called? Agates? Immies? Guppies?

Outdoors, I spent other happy hours hurling a pink rubber ball at the steps of my house in a game I still called stoopball because I had come from the Bronx, a place full of stone steps that the Dutch had called *stoeps* and we called stoops. If the ball hit squarely on the edge of a stoop, it went flying across the street and you probably got a home run, or else a run home if the ball broke a window on what your neighbors hadn't known was the center-field wall.

It used to be a charming bit of Americana to show a small nervous boy at the front door of a house that had just been given new ventilation. Only once, in the summer of 1942, was I that boy and for several tense seconds I wondered if the charm would ever kick in.

"You're the Wood boy, aren't you?" said Mrs. Wren, and Wood began turning to jelly, for Charles Osgood Wood III was my name.

This was my chance to be someone else and prevent her from tracing the criminal to the family across the street, but I didn't think quickly enough.

"Yes, I am, Mrs. Wren," I said, "and I'm really sorry about the window. I'll pay for it."

If ever there had been an empty gesture, that was it.

"That's all right," she said. "It could have happened to anyone."

It could have happened to anyone hurling a rubber ball at a step directly across the street; but her reply was typical of the good feeling that pervaded America that year. Mrs. Wren must have known that it would be wrong to turn on me when we were fighting the Axis together.

"You're an altar boy, aren't you?" she said. "At Our Lady of Lourdes."

"Yes, ma'am, I am," I said, giving her my most angelic expression.

"You're a good talker, Charles," she said. "You'll make a good lawyer."

And wasn't that just what America needed: one more lawyer. Of course, I did end up talking for a living, but only in the court of public opinion.

Scene from *The Mark of Zorro*

Not Quite Huck Finn

I SOMETIMES WONDER how I went into a business as warlike as commercial broadcasting, because in spite of breaking Mrs. Wren's window and a few other loopy lapses, I was always a good boy. Year after year, I passed up inviting chances to misbehave because a quirk in my character left me endlessly eager to make people happy. I probably should have stayed at Our Lady of Lourdes and worked as a play-by-play announcer for Mass. And I would have done it with style:

Cool, clear day in the cathedral. Heavily Catholic crowd. Seats are packed with Holy Trinity fans . . . And here comes Father Hickey, just brought up from the

Tyson diocese, where his number of consecutive confessions broke the Eastern Shore record . . . He's picking up the wine and mixing it with the water. Not much water, I must say.

Years later, when I was a student at Fordham University, life imitated this little boyhood fantasy: On the campus radio station, WFUV, I narrated daily Mass from the Blue Chapel. I don't think my rating was particularly high, even though the show was in morning drive time.

In those boyhood years, I was already feeling a passion for radio, but my strongest passion was to make people happy. If an American boy today were primarily motivated by such a desire, he might be sent to a psychiatrist to find the cause of such abnormal behavior.

"Charles, have you *always* had this strange compulsion to make people happy?" the psychiatrist would say.

"Yes, always!" I would reply. "I'll bet you like hearing that, right? But please tell me if there's something you'd *rather* hear. I've never wanted to make *a single person* unhappy, unless you count Hitler."

"And how do you *feel* about it?"

"I feel terrific! I really hope that's the right answer, because I want you to be happy with my score."

"But isn't it possible that this strange compulsion of yours is . . . well, an overcompensation for something?"

"I don't know what that means, but I'll be happy to learn."

"What I mean is deep inside you maybe you're angry or jealous about something. For example, perhaps you feel penis envy."

"But I'm a *boy*."

"*Other* boys' penises."

⌒

59

When I was nine, there was no limit to my decency, except perhaps on the day I did some freelance upholstery work with scissors much sharper than my mind.

While reading to Mary Ann and me one evening, my father had let a spark from his cigarette fall on the armrest of our living-room chair and burn a hole in the fabric. My resourceful mother had cut a small square from the back of the chair to repair the arm, an act that seemed like so much fun that I also took some scissors and made a few slashes in the back of the chair. I felt that my mother no longer needed the chair; and after those slashes, I might have been right.

"Charlie," she said, "did you or Mary Ann make those slashes in the chair?"

I loved my sister, but I couldn't give her credit for such artistry.

"*I* did it, Mom," I proudly replied. "Pretty neat, huh, the way I made my initial—*your* initial too. A *W* wasn't easy, y'know. Are you proud?"

She was silent for a moment, seeking a proper response to creative stupidity. And then she found it:

"Are you *mad*?"

"Oh no, Mom, I'm not mad at anyone."

People have come to use "mad" for angry, though its true meaning is insane. Between us that day, my mother and I were both.

60

Reupholstering that chair—*de*upholstering it, actually—was innocent dumbness, not delinquency. But there *was* one memorable exception to my life as a Goody Two-shoes, and incredibly, it was when I used those shoes to run away from home. Of course, I did it in the nicest possible way; and my running away might even have been an acceptable response to something that had happened at 3504 Edgewood Road.

My unforgettable flight was the climax of a series of events that followed my seeing a movie called *The Mark of Zorro*—and then living it.

One of my boyhood pastimes was telling the story of a movie I had just seen to anyone who was interested, and even to people who weren't. Happily for me, the person who most enjoyed my cinematic renditions was a girl down the block named Sue Einstein, on whom I had a crush.

Although Sue's name was Einstein, she probably was no relation to the other one, because her mind was nothing to write home about. Her face, however, called for an international cable: She had big dark eyes, a slightly turned-up nose, and a bow of a mouth so fetching that there was no need for intelligence to come from it.

Week after week, I wooed Sue Einstein not with poetry but plots. A few days before seeing a revival of *The Mark of Zorro*, I had seen a film called *Pride of the Yankees*; and my dramatizing it for Sue had combined my love for movies, baseball, and her into a truly winged synopsis.

"And so, Lou Gehrig is standing there in Yankee Stadium and everyone knows he's dying, so—"

"Dying of what?" said Sue.

"A baseball disease called three strikes."

Sue laughed. "I think you've gotten that wrong, Charlie," she said. "There's no such disease called *three strikes*."

"Oh, yeah there is," I said. "Lou Gehrig goes to a big clinic somewhere and he asks the doctor, 'Is it three strikes, Doc?' and the doctor says, 'I'm afraid so, Lou.'"

"Gee, I never *heard* of that disease."

"Lou wishes he'd never heard of it too."

"Maybe he should've gone to Johns Hopkins."

"So listen, Sue," I said. "This is the part that'll kill ya. At

61

the end of the picture, he's invited to Yankee Stadium 'cause that's where you go when you're dyin'. And he stands there at the microphone in the stadium and he says, 'Today . . . today . . . I consider myself . . . consider myself . . . the luckiest man . . . luckiest man . . . on the face of the earth . . . the face of the earth.' "

"Why does he say everything twice?"

"It must've been the disease."

⌒

There was something I wanted to say just once to Sue. Because I had seen many films with romantic heroes, I was possessed by the dopey notion to ask her to be my girl. Although at nine I was an impressive distance from puberty and had never kissed a nonrelative, I now felt driven to put Sue in a bond that might have been ridiculous even in India.

My problem was not that Sue might have already been taken; few girls of nine were engaged, even in the wilder parts of Baltimore. My problem was I lacked the courage to ask her, for I feared her answer might be "Are you out of your *mind*?" And my answer to *that* would have been "Yes."

And so, after telling her *Pride of the Yankees*, I sought the courage of Lou Gehrig, but in vain. I remained the most dumbly hopeful boy on the face of the earth.

Although I certainly had charmed Sue Einstein with that presentation of *Pride of the Yankees*, I did more than just dispense charm after seeing *The Mark of Zorro*: I began to *live* the story as if I were Zorro, who had been played by Hollywood's handsomest leading man, Tyrone Power, the major inspiration for my wanting to make Sue my girl.

In this film, Zorro handled his own public relations by simply spreading his initial around. No songs or press releases about how great he was were necessary; Zorro just rode all over the countryside, a mad monogrammer marking Z's on the walls of places and daring the police to catch him. A lot of people also weren't particularly fond of him, and not because of any anti-graffiti laws.

I don't remember the precise composition of Zorro's enemies, but they included corrupt public officials, so he could have been riding in New Jersey, though I'm pretty sure it was California. I do clearly remember that Zorro was a hero whose hobby was defacing property—a brave though slightly insane rider in a swirling black cape who went around taunting his enemies with his sword and sometimes making holes in them too. He never wrote ZORRO on things, not because he had a short attention span but because Z was enough: Not too many lunatics in black were riding around with names

63

that started with Z. He was lucky not to have had a name like Osgood. A circle on a building wall might have been taken for a place to connect a hose.

⌐

Aflame from the tale of this masked avenger, I decided to stop being a Baltimore cherub and to start putting Z's on things, even though I couldn't think of anything to avenge. I was moving up, or maybe down, from my work with upholstery in which I had initialed the back of that chair. From W, I skipped X and Y and went directly to Z.

I clearly wasn't the brightest self-promoter in the East, because Z didn't happen to be the first letter of my name. However, the pointlessness of my crusade never stayed my right arm, which used a crayon, a pencil, and the cold steel of an oyster pick to put Z's all over our house. I was Tyrone Power with a utensil and a Crayola—undaunted, unafraid, and uninvolved with my brain. My masterstroke was making a Z in our living-room couch, a Z that nicely revealed the material below. Thoughtfully, I sliced the letter in the *back* of the couch, where I felt my mother would prefer it.

It wasn't long before I discovered exactly who Zorro's enemies were: my parents. Of course, the destruction could have been worse: I could have been inspired by having seen *Genghis Khan*.

"Charles," said my mother one day after making a citizen's arrest, "first it's a *W* in a chair and now a *Z* in the couch—and all over the place!"

"At least he's through with the alphabet," my father said.

"But—but . . . can you tell me what on earth got into your *head* to make you put *Z*'s all over the house?" said my understandably bewildered mother.

"I'm afraid there's nothing in his head," my father said, an insult I decided to let pass while wondering what Tyrone Power would have done. He wouldn't have been posting graffiti in Baltimore, of course, where the land was ruled not by a Spanish governor but an Irish mayor.

"Charles," said my father, "you will have to be punished for this." And he directed my mother, the designated spanker, to come to bat.

"I don't need the blindfold," I told her, squaring my shoulders while thinking about a spy being shot.

But it wasn't my mother's custom to blindfold me for spankings: She believed that the criminal should participate in the spanking as much as he could.

Once the Son of Zorro had retired, I returned to being the prince of peace. I was, however, still deeply involved with crayons because I loved to eat them, as well as other things with questionable nutritional value like pencil erasers and little balls of paper. As if a harbinger of my future career, I was a very oral child.

I did not, of course, always *eat* little balls of paper: Sometimes I put them into other holes in my head. One day, to her dismay, my mother discovered that one of my ears needed a Roto-Rooter and called our family doctor, Milton Nibbler, who came to our house.

"That boy chewed some paper and put it in his *ear*," she said to Dr. Nibbler, whose name indicated that he was the ideal man for this particular condition.

"He did *what*?" said Dr. Nibbler, starting to laugh.

"Put *paper* in his *ear*."

"Marvelous!" said the laughing doctor, taking a break from professional detachment. "Put paper . . . in his . . . *ear*!"

In all my years in radio, I doubt I have ever entertained anyone as much as I entertained Dr. Nibbler that day. I have had the listener's ear, but that day my own was better.

His presence as an audience in my home tells you that I grew up in an era as vanished as the Napoleonic: a doctor making a house call because a boy had used his ear as a trash can. Today, a boy could swallow the entire sports section and one of the doctor's nurses would say, "Bring him in next Thursday at four. If he vomits, press six."

My oral disposition did lead me to do some throwing up myself one day, but it wasn't anything as bland as paper. One Sunday, my parents took Mary Ann and me to the center of Baltimore for a seafood dinner at Miller Brothers restaurant, which served things that fit only in my mouth. About ten minutes after we had begun to enjoy fine plates of fish, I suddenly felt an urgent need to have another look at it. In the men's room, standing lovingly beside me while I reversed the meal, Dad wondered what I had eaten that was purple. I had to confess to him that, just before coming downtown, I had eaten a purple crayon. I should have chosen one that matched the flounder.

67

The week after this memorable two-way meal, it happened: the event that sent me and Mary Ann traveling the *wrong* way—away from home. Huck Finn would not have been impressed by the way we did it. The police certainly weren't.

Me and my sister Mary Ann

—✍—

There's No Place Like
a Station House

SOMEWHAT SHORT OF legitimate hobbies, Mary Ann and I liked to have fun with the telephone by calling people and places we should not have been calling. I didn't realize it then, primarily because I was busy being a jerk, but these calls were the first development of my communications skills; and if I had continued in their direction, I might have become a telemarketer or even ended in a place where I was given a nickel to make just one call. Yes, calls were a nickel then, half the price of a loaf of bread.

The harmless calls that Mary Ann and I made were to some of the ballplayers we loved, the Orioles who were listed in the Baltimore directory. Can you imagine trying to call Mike Piazza today? You couldn't get through to his tailor; but the Baltimore telephone directory of 1942 had the number for the best center fielder in the International League, the Orioles' Loyola Joe Mellendick.

"Hi, is this Loyola Joe Mellendick?" I said one afternoon.

"Yeah," said a gruff voice. "Who's *this*?"

"Charlie and Mary Ann," I said, protecting us by withholding our last name.

"Charlie and Mary Ann *who*?"

"Your two biggest fans."

Any player whose two biggest fans were kids who played telephone games was a man who needed to reappraise his following.

"Kids . . . it's . . . it's really nice of you to call," he said.

"So how're things, Loyola Joe?" I said.

"Well, right now I got a little headache."

"You must've had one in the Newark game."

"Well . . . you get days like that."

"Right. You don't usually stink."

"Thanks very much for the call."

Those calls were enjoyed by the players, but Mary Ann and I had another call in our repertoire that gave the person who answered all the delight of hearing from a collection agency. Because our telephone number was FOrest 1750, we often got calls intended for the American Sugar Company, which was SOuth 1750. And so, we felt obliged to stay in touch with the American Sugar Company by calling from time to time.

These calls were Mary Ann's times to shine. The moment that the phone at SOuth 1750 was answered, she coquettishly said, "Hello, *sugar?*" Sometimes, her inflection was a question to her true love and sometimes it was an outpouring from her own heart: "*Hello*, sugar!" It was possible, of course, that American Sugar found Mary Ann's performance less delicious than I did. There is no accounting for taste.

One afternoon while Mary Ann was sweet-talking a stranger, our mother walked into the room.

"Who are you two *calling?*" she said.

That should have been *whom*, but this was probably not the moment to correct her.

"Oh—no one," said Mary Ann, thinking quickly but not quickly enough.

"Would you like to try another answer?" our mother said.

"We had to call a sugar company," I said. "For homework."

"For *homework?*"

"Yeah, we're studying food and my assignment is

sugar—that's a better one than bacon fat—and I'm supposed to find out everything I can about it."

I was always a fast talker, even when I didn't know what I was saying, and this was one of those times.

"Well, you'll give your report to your father tonight. He'll want to know all about sugar. Especially how it affects his phone bill."

⌒

That evening, in a doubleheader, the two of us were spanked. My spanking for having been a two-bit Zorro was understandable; and I would even have understood a spanking for coloring my stomach before Sunday dinner. But a spanking for Mary Ann's auditioning for radio seemed like overkill, even though that word didn't exist in 1942.

"That spanking was just *unfair*," she said to me the next day.

"It sure was," I replied. "Mom didn't even ask the American Sugar people if we were *bothering* them."

"I think we should teach her a lesson," she said.

"What do you think she'd like to learn?"

"Let's run away!"

"From *home*?"

"Where *else* are we?"

⌒

Amazingly, the following Saturday morning, we two thoroughly decent kids did just that: We ran away. To be accurate, we walked away, and perhaps a bit too spontaneously. Because we had consulted no travel agent to help us plan the trip, when we reached Copley Avenue, we discovered that we had almost no money, just some small change from our allowances.

A boy running away, with or without his sister, is an honored American tradition. Huck Finn had no money either. However, you probably could have gotten farther without funds in the Missouri of 1850 than the Maryland of 1942.

"Let's count our money," I said.

That didn't take long: $2.25.

"I don't think you can run away very far with two and a quarter," I said.

"You want to go back for some?" said Mary Ann.

"I don't think that's the way you're supposed to do it."

"I guess it's not."

"Hey, I've *got* it!" I said. "Let's turn in some *bottles*!"

"We don't have any."

"Let's *find* some!"

At once, the two wee fugitives began a desperate recycling drive along Copley Avenue, going into trash cans for bottles that could be redeemed for as much as five cents. Redemption for *us* might be harder, but we bravely ignored thoughts of the trouble we would be in if we ever decided to go home.

While Mary Ann and I drifted away to collect bottles, hoping that no neighbor would call our home, our dog Inky followed us, a touch that Norman Rockwell would have used. Though Inky was a mutt, he was still smarter than we were: After staying with us for just a few blocks, he decided that two wandering bottle collectors would be lucky to feed themselves, let alone *him*. Sensing that Mary Ann and I were already lost just five blocks away, Inky suddenly turned back for home.

74

"I hope Inky doesn't tell them we're gone," said Mary Ann.

"They may figure that out for themselves," I said. "They're pretty smart."

The same description did not apply to a couple of kids seeking liberty from Liberty Heights. We were able to redeem several bottles at a grocery store, but we still lacked the financing to light out into the territory, as Huck Finn called it. We could barely glow in Baltimore.

After walking down Edgewood Road and then Copley, Mary Ann and I found ourselves on Yosemite Avenue, a fitting route for a trip into the wilderness; next was Sequoia Avenue, which also had the call of the West. However, before we hit the Grand Canyon, we saw a movie house, the Ambassador, playing a new film called *Holiday Inn*. The afternoon show was about to start and we felt we deserved a break from our great trek.

"But they won't let kids in alone," said Mary Ann. "We'd better get a parent."

We would probably be needing new parents anyway if we ever went home, so we auditioned a mother.

"Lady," I boldly said to a woman approaching the box office, "would you take us in with you? Here's our money."

I gave her two quarters.

"Where is your mother?" she said.

"She's . . . having an operation," I found myself saying.

"Oh, my. I hope she'll be all right."

"Oh, she's all right, right now—I mean, as soon as they operate."

"What's wrong with her, if I may ask?"

"It's got something to do with her body. So she told us to see a movie until the doctor calls us."

How the doctor could have called us in the theater was a detail that, like all the rest of our flight, I hadn't completely thought through. Dr. Nibbler would have had another good laugh.

"Of course I'll take you in," she said. "And then I'll take you to the hospital."

"Oh, no!" I said. "I mean, we don't know which one it is. Baltimore's got so many, you know."

"It may not even be a hospital," said Mary Ann with a flair for fiction even weaker than mine.

Holiday Inn, with Bing Crosby and Fred Astaire, was so good that we stayed to see it again. Of course, we also might have stayed to see a travelogue about Toledo because we had nowhere to go.

The film was full of splendid songs that made me feel life would still be wonderful even if my parents gave me away. In one of the songs, Bing Crosby was sitting at a piano and dreaming of a white Christmas with a tune so infectious that I kept humming it after the second show had ended. Sue Einstein would melt when I hummed it to her. To do that, however, I would have to see her again, which might not happen if Mary Ann and I were sent to the Baltimore Home for Idiot Children.

This thought was so melancholy that I soothed myself with a couple of candy bars. The snack bar didn't sell crayons.

When we left the theater, streetlights were glowing in the dusk and we were suddenly afraid.

"I'm scared, Miss Duffy," I said.

"Likewise, I'm sure," she replied, quoting from *Duffy's Tavern*, a radio show we both loved.

"We need Superman or Mandrake the Magician," I said,

fearing that the man we most needed would be Mister District Attorney.

"Wanna go back?"

"I dunno. Do you?"

"Aren't we devils?" she said.

That one was from *Truth or Consequences*. And consequences would certainly be coming.

"Hey, I know what!" I said. "Let's go to *Lusko's*! I want some ice cream. With Hershey syrup."

"Lusko's is the other way," said Mary Ann. "And we don't have enough money. And they'd catch us there."

"So you don't think it's a good idea?"

"Forget about Lusko's," she said. "We better figure out where we're gonna spend the night."

"You think we should stay away that long?" I said.

"Well, nobody runs away just for a *movie*. I mean, *that* doesn't count as running away."

Baltimore's two cutest fugitives were now approaching the edge of Hanlon Park.

"Hey, we could go sleep in the park!" I said.

"Icch!" said Mary Ann. "You remember what Mom said about rolling around on the lawn?"

"Mary Ann, don't be dumb! You don't have to listen to your mother when you're *running away*. That's what running away *is*. Hey, I got another great idea!"

"That one wasn't so great."

"We can sleep in a church!"

"Are they *open*?" she said.

"They're *always* open and we're *Catholic*."

"I know we are," she said. "I guess it's lucky to be Catholic when you're running away."

"We'll have to get up for Mass," I said, "but I know how to do that. I do that all the time at Lourdes."

"Maybe they'll say a Mass for *us*."

I was an altar boy—I was about to become a *former* altar boy—who often carried the heavy missal and lit the incense at the day's first Mass. At dawn in the church, I sometimes put extra incense on the charcoal to make the mist more like a smokescreen the Pacific fleet might use. And a smokescreen was what Mary Ann and I needed now.

Like two small criminals, we walked on in search of sanctuary. By now it was dark and we were starting to shiver from the cold. To keep up our morale, I began a little routine that, for no particular reason, Mary Ann and I liked to do from time to time: I gallantly presented my right arm to her while saying in a warmly inviting voice, *"Alice."* And then she took the arm, even though her name wasn't Alice, and the two of us began to promenade like a couple of swells.

I never knew where that "Alice" came from. Perhaps from the film star Alice Faye, who was a distant cousin of ours; or perhaps from Alice of Wonderland, who would have been appropriate because we were certainly down the Rabbit-Hole now.

Whenever Mary Ann and I did this routine at home or school, it was charming; but it had less charm when we were running away, so we turned to lifting our spirits by playing one of our favorite games: guessing the names of movie stars from hearing their initials.

"Okay, who is C. G.?" said Mary Ann.

"Clark Gable," I said.

"Wrong."

"*Wrong*? Clark Gable has *other* initials?"

"I'm not thinking of him."

"I don't *care*, I *am*."

"Charlie, it has to be what *I'm* thinking of."

"Unless there's two. Mary Ann, you used to be good at this game."

"Well, there *are* two and this is the *other* one. It's somebody *else*."

"You know what? I'm sorry I ran away with *you*."

"Who *else* did you have?"

"Willard Wallaby."

"They'd be *happy* if he ran away."

"I still say it's Clark Gable."

"You know what, Charlie? I'm not having so much fun anymore. And it happens to be *Cary Grant*."

"Yeah, I guess his initials are C. G."

"You *guess*? How'd you ever get into the fourth grade?"

"Hey, let's stop fighting, okay? It's not so great to keep fighting when you're running away."

"Yeah, we better stop till we get someplace."

"Okay. T. P. And I'll take only one person that fits."

I was ready to accept only Tyrone Power when a car pulled up to the curb and a voice cried out, "Just where do you two think you're going?"

What a coincidence: It was our mother. It didn't take me long to realize that no mere hairbrush would be sufficient to spank us for this one; Mom would have to move up to garden supplies.

"Hi, Mom!" I breezily said, deciding to take a shot at pretending that nothing had happened. However, she had a posse in the car who had been helping her look for us. I was particularly happy to see them because their presence meant that Mary Ann and I would not be killed in the car. That event would take place later in the home from which we had recently emigrated.

"Have you two children lost your *minds*?" said my mother rhetorically.

"We didn't mean it, Mom," I said, a statement not rich in logic. How do you run away from home and not mean it?

"Do you know that I have the *police* looking for you?" she said.

"You can tell them we're found," Mary Ann brightly said.

"No, *you're* going to tell them."

"We'll phone them as soon as we get home," my sister said, knowing how good she was on the phone.

"No," said my mother, "you'll tell them in *person*."

And then, in an inspired defense, Mary Ann tried to save us by tying us to the great sweep of Christianity.

"Mom, St. Teresa of Avila ran away to the Crusades," she said. "She even tried to talk her brother into going with her."

"You planned to spread the word of the Lord in that *movie?*" my mother said.

Nevertheless, it was a nice Hail Mary play by Mary Ann.

⌒

I hadn't planned for my first visit to a police station to be as a wanted man, but that was my identification when my mother led Mary Ann and me into a precinct near our home.

"These are the children who were missing," she told the desk sergeant. "They've come to apologize."

I wondered about trying a plea bargain, having the sergeant tell my mother to spank only one of us, perhaps Mary Ann; but I sensed that my mother expected a double confession.

"We're sorry, Captain," I said.

Happy to be promoted, the sergeant smiled and said, "I'm sure you are. Just don't do it again."

"Oh, we won't," said Mary Ann. "There's no place like home."

This remark should have annoyed me because *I* was the one who was supposed to quote from movies, but I knew that she was using her mouth to save another part.

⌒

Running away from home had been a childish thing to do; but just a few weeks later, I proved that I was really a man.

I had always gone out of my way to avoid physical confrontations. I didn't like the idea of hitting anyone. On an even deeper philosophical level, I didn't like the idea of anyone hitting me. However, one morning, just like America, I was the victim of a sneak attack.

On my front porch that day—the porch with four white columns on blocks of stone—I was stacking newspapers that I was about to deliver, pausing from time to time to study the news of the war. I was happy to see that Field Marshal Montgomery was still chasing Rommel across Egypt and that B-17s were bombing Italy and France. Suddenly, a boy from down the street named Harry sneaked up behind me, a boy who'd always thought it was funny to play such jokes as sticking out his leg when you walked by. Harry was almost as funny as Rommel.

On this particular day, while I was holding a big stack of newspapers, Harry amusingly punched me in my back and knocked me to my knees, the kind of rabbit punch that was everything America was fighting against. It was a date that for me will live in infamy, even though I've forgotten what date it was.

In what was the low point of my life, unless being captured by my mother's posse was lower, I went sprawling on my face and the newspapers went flying all over the porch. Jumping up, I was so enraged that I made an exception to my feeling about violence and belted Harry in the face. I hit him so hard that he went backward over the porch railing and into the juniper bushes, like someone John Wayne had just hit in a film I would be telling to Sue Einstein. Still shaking with rage, I was prepared for my enemy to come back and disassemble my body parts, but he just walked away.

The next time I saw Harry, he was a convert to oral humor and I never had another fight, with him or anyone else. Like Rocky Marciano, I retired undefeated with a record of 1 and 0. I had shown that boy that it wasn't wise to mess with an American, whether that messing was striking a blow for the Rising Sun or against the *Sun* of Baltimore.

83

Plant a Victory Garden poster

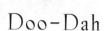

Doo-Dah

I WILL NEVER forget the epiphany I experienced the day that the Japanese attacked Pearl Harbor. It came before the news arrived from Hawaii, and had less to do with the military than the music. That afternoon, Mary Ann and I were seated together in the main assembly hall of Our Lady of Lourdes, at a musical about the South that was part of the church's annual fund-raising carnival.

A church was the right place for an epiphany, and mine that day was hearing the songs of Stephen Foster and instantly falling in love with them. As the show went on, I found myself singing, "Oh Susannah, don't you cry for me," and, "Oh the sun shines bright on my old Kentucky home," and, "Doo-dah, doo-dah, all de doo-dah day."

"Charles," said Sister Serena Branson, paying a special visit to my seat, "you have a lovely voice, but perhaps right now you should let those on*stage* perform."

"Sorry, Sister," I said.

Sunday, December 7, 1941, was exactly one month before my ninth birthday and one month after Mary Ann's eighth, but I suspect she was more mature than I. Suspect? Her hobbies were not snacking on crayons, making stink bombs, and reducing her hearing with small paper balls.

"What's *wrong* with you?" whispered Mary Ann.

"I gotta sing that music!" I said.

I wasn't going to say *Sorry, Sister*, to *her*.

For the next hour, I felt an emotional connection to Stephen Foster. He had died of alcoholism in Baltimore and I was getting drunk there on his music, intoxicated by the melodies and moved to laughter by some of the words. *Oh it rained all night the day we left/The weather it was dry* struck me as the funniest thing I'd ever heard. Of course, I hadn't heard much.

I wanted that show to go on forever, but it came to an end—and unforgettably. While the chorus was singing "Jeannie with the Light Brown Hair," Sister Serena suddenly walked onto the stage. The song didn't seem to need a nun, especially one with black hair, but of course all this was new to me.

"Children," she said after stopping the singing, "I'm afraid I have alarming news: Our naval base at Pearl Harbor has been attacked by the Japanese. Please go right home and tell your parents, in case they haven't heard. We will have school as usual tomorrow. Let us pray for America."

When I left the church that Sunday singing "Doo-dah, doo-dah," I was grooving in an America about to change more profoundly than it had since the Civil War, which half of Baltimore felt had been won by the wrong team.

On the day in 1939 when my family had moved from the Bronx to Baltimore, I felt we had come to Paradise, but now a war had come there too. The moment I had arrived at that brown house on Edgewood Road, Mary Ann and I had run out to the little lawn behind it and gotten high on the grass, for grass in the Bronx had been the outfield at Yankee Stadium. We had gazed at the clouds, looking for shapes, and sucked in the fresh air and giddily rolled around on the grass. After a while, I had even started chewing it.

"Charlie!" my mother had cried. "Stop eating that grass!"

"I'm not swallowing it, Mom," I had replied.

"Well, take it out of your mouth and stop *rolling around* in it! *Dogs* run around out there!"

I hadn't minded sharing the lawn with dogs or any other wildlife, but now the war had brought a cloud to Paradise. As the year went on, I devoted myself to fighting the war in three different ways, all of which were more than quixotic: They were dumb. However, as a loyal American, I had to do what I could to keep Liberty Heights correctly named.

⌒

The first way I fought was to try to make our victory garden a winner instead of the loser it had been since we first planted it. All spring, while Mary Ann watered the garden to grow all the things I left on my plate, I kept trying to think of something that would actually be edible. I would be in better shape to fight the Germans and Japs if I didn't have to spit out what had come up.

Suddenly, one day in July, inspiration struck: I would plant the seeds of everything I liked: strawberries, watermelons, apples, oranges, peaches, and pears. Most of these grew on trees, of course, so the growing would be a definite challenge; but I was full of the gritty optimism with which Winston Churchill was leading the Allies to victory.

At a garden supplies store, I used my allowance to buy all these seeds, which I planted in an extension of the victory garden that probably should have been called surrender soil. For the rest of the summer, bursting with hope, I watered my extension, even after the rain. At least I had stopped short of trying to produce Baltimore's first banana tree.

⌐

My other two ways of fighting the war unfortunately might have encouraged the enemy, because they involved Willard Wallaby. To help defend America, Willard and I did scientific work as original as that being done under the stadium at the University of Chicago. Did Enrico Fermi ever unlock the secret of a stink bomb?

Proudly poised at my Gilbert chemistry set to begin making weapons of mass disgust to waft at the enemy, I said, "Just wait'll the Germans and Japs get a whiff of these!"

"The Germans and Japs might not be coming to Baltimore right away," Willard said. "They might go to Philly first, so it could be a while, an' the stink only hangs around for a few minutes. I mean, you gotta use a stink bomb right away or it goes bad an' the enemy is just gettin' a breath of fresh air."

"Hey, that's something we can tell Sister Marie in science!" I said. "A stink bomb is the only thing that smells *better* when it goes *bad*!"

I should have been under that stadium at the University of Chicago.

The Gilbert Company had given no directions for how to make and sustain stink bombs; in an annoyingly scientific tone, it had said only that sulfur dioxide gas smelled like rotten eggs. Willard and I wondered if we should skip the gas and go directly to the eggs.

"You think the Germans have a Gilbert?" said Willard.

"I wouldn't be surprised," I said. "They're pretty smart. They invented oxygen and stuff like that. There are lots of 'em in Baltimore, y' know."

"I think those ones are on our side," said Willard.

"Well, we'd better keep an eye on *them* too."

After considerable rancid testing in the name of freedom, Willard and I learned to heat a spoonful of sulfur powder over a flame so that it became sulfur dioxide gas and smelled like rotten eggs; but the weapon *was* only a gas and not containable in anything that could be saved and thrown at the enemy. The scientific challenge was huge: Unless the Germans invaded my house at the precise moment the gas was released, our work would not be a significant contribution to the war effort.

"Harry says we can make hydrogen sulfide gas that's even *rottener*," said Willard one day.

"What's the point?" I said. "It'll still just stink for *us*."

Our work with stink bombs, though totally futile, was still impressive for the intensity of the muddled thought that we gave to it. Our next homeland defense made more sense, although it would have been hard to come up with anything that made less. Rather than rest on our stink-bomb work, Willard and I set out to memorize the designs of enemy planes, not just bombers but fighters too. We didn't know, of course, that the only fighters that could have attacked the United States would have had to sneak in from Canada, Mexico, or Bermuda. Thinking that Stukas, Messerschmitts, and Zeroes might fly past Chesapeake Bay without being spotted, we studied photographs of these and other enemy planes so we could call the government the moment we saw one over Edgewood Road.

"Maybe we don't have to learn this one," said Willard, holding up a picture of a Zero. "I don't think a Zero can make it to Baltimore. Cleveland at the most; I mean, it's comin' from *Japan*."

"Yeah, we may be a little out of Japanese range," I said. "Let's work on the Stukas and Messerschmitts."

"You really think *they* can come over?"

"Didn't Doolittle hit Tokyo with B-24s? We don't want to be surprised like that. Okay now, what's this one?"

I held up a picture of a plane.

"Messerschmitt 109!" said Willard triumphantly.

"Wrong, it's a P-38; that was a trick. Willard, you gotta do better or Baltimore'll be *all* Germans. Any day now, they could be comin' in low over Chesapeake Bay."

And suddenly I found myself singing, "Bet my money on a bobtail nag, somebody bet on the bay."

"That a new song?" said Willard.

"I heard it at church."

"Whadda ya mean, 'bet on the bay'? A race at Chesapeake or somethin'?"

"I'm gonna ask Matilda Dietsch tomorrow."

He started to laugh. "Matilda Dietsch? That's the goofiest name I ever heard," said Willard Wallaby.

"I'd tell her that, but she'd hit me with an evil spell. She's that kind of woman. At least, I *think* she's a woman."

⌒

The next day, at my piano lesson, I decided to skip the question about Chesapeake Bay because I realized that Stephen Foster was too hip for Matilda K. Dietsch. Mendelssohn was too hip for her too. She was an elderly lady who came to my house once a week to give piano lessons to Mary Ann and me. At least, she *seemed* elderly to us; she might have been almost forty. Dressed always in a suit, hat, shoes, handbag, and even umbrella that were coordinated to perfection, she was a no-nonsense teacher who wasn't ideal for me, because nonsense was my major. Mary Ann and I did learn well from her; but while we were learning, Matilda K. Dietsch sometimes made me consider switching to the kazoo.

Her lessons were planned like military campaigns and were almost as much fun. First, I had to practice endless scales and then endless chords; then she listened to me play a piece that she had assigned the previous week. I remember that I once did a particularly moving rendition of "The Happy Farmer," one of the many pieces I played too slowly so I would have time to find the notes.

"*Round* those fingers, Charles," she kept saying. "*Round* those fingers."

"I'm *trying*, Miss Dietsch," I would say. "I guess I just have flat hands."

"*Everyone* has flat hands. *Schumann* would want you to round them."

"Schumann was German, right?"

"That's right."

"Well, they're the enemy now."

"No, Schumann is your friend and so am I and we both want you to round those hands."

A bigger problem than the contour of my fingers was the length of my legs: I was short at nine—Mary Ann was the tall one—and could barely reach the pedals. This missed connection, however, probably improved my playing because the piano had three pedals and I could never remember what each of them did.

"And *tempo, tempo*, Charles," she kept saying. "The farmer is supposed to be *happy*. One presumes he has harvested a good crop."

"What does he grow?"

"That's not important. Now for next week, you will learn 'Traumerei.'"

"Is it a fast one?"

"Not when played correctly, it isn't. It's a reverie."

"A what?"

"Like a dream. And if you play it well, I just might give you another reward card."

Presented for good performance at the piano, Miss Dietsch's reward cards were pictures of composers with brief descriptions of their lives, but getting one no longer was a thrill for me. My first had been a Beethoven for playing his "Minuet in G" without once leaving the key. Appreciating its value, I had tried to trade it on the open card market at school, but discovered that a Beethoven didn't bring even a Vince DiMaggio. Schumann was a *lesser* composer who wouldn't have brought more than Triple A.

⌐

In the fall, Miss Dietsch arranged for all her students to give a concert at Baltimore's Peabody Conservatory. Deciding to play through strength, I passed up "Für Elise," a piece with both too many sharps and too much speed, and went with my signature song, "The Happy Farmer." To prepare for the concert, I practiced the piece so much that my Happy Farmer was giddy and there was a definite curve to my hands that hadn't been there before.

"Hey, Mary Ann," I said one day. "You wanna see *round hands*? Take a look at *those*."

I then played "The Happy Farmer" with no more than a half dozen mistakes.

"Miss Dietsch wants you to get the notes right too," said Mary Ann.

"One or the other," I said. "I can't do both."

95

My father made certain that he was home from his travels for the Christmas concert by the rounded little hands of Matilda K. Dietsch's students. How proudly he and my mother looked at the program announcing that Mary Ann's "Humoresque" would be played third and my "Happy Farmer" would be next to last.

"Charlie is next to closing," my father told my mother. "In vaudeville, that was always the star spot."

Perhaps his son should have been playing at Minsky's, for in this big concert hall I was feeling even more nervous than when I had to tell the police that my runaway days were over.

Trying to calm my nerves by talking, I told Mary Ann, "Go get 'em, Mary Ann! *You* can do it! You can go *all the way*! Go *get* 'em!"

Going all the way to get 'em might not have been what Sol Hurok had told Vladimir Horowitz, but it was from the heart, and the nerves.

"Thank you, Charlie," she said. "That's very sweet."

"And if you mess up, there'll still be a chance for me to save the family name."

A few minutes later, Mary Ann played and did well, though I would have taken "Humoresque" more slowly.

As I fought to reconcile feelings of wanting to play and being terrified to do it, each of the other students performed. When the last student sat down to play and I was still waiting, all I could think was that Dietsch had done something wonderful: She had made me the grand finale.

But suddenly, she was standing before the parents to thank them for coming. If I was to be a grand finale, it would be for some *other* concert.

"They *forgot* you," said my mother, as if I had missed that fact, and I started to cry.

Hearing my sobs, Miss Dietsch quickly came over to me and said, "What's the matter, Charles?"

I was crying too hard to speak, but my mother said to her, "You forgot to call his name."

"Of course!" said Miss Dietsch, who perhaps had been

96

trying to brighten the concert by leaving me out of it. Turning to the people who were starting to leave, she cried in the voice of an air-raid warden, "Ladies and gentlemen, will everyone please come back! Everyone please come back to your seats!"

In bewilderment, the members of the audience returned to the hall.

"Ladies and gentlemen, let me apologize for a truly regrettable mistake," Miss Dietsch said. "I forgot to have Charles Wood III play."

Yes, as I've said, my full name was Charles Osgood Wood III; I was carrying the elegant load of precisely the same name as my father and grandfather. With a name so patrician, I probably should not have been wiping my face on my sleeve when I began to play, a half-pint Horowitz with a postnasal drip.

I don't remember how well I played "The Happy Farmer" that day, but my execution didn't matter because it was a no-lose performance: The parents hearing it were feeling as sorry for me as I had been feeling for myself. Not one of them cared if my fingers were round or squared.

When I had finished the piece, I received the greatest response of the evening. It was, in fact, a standing ovation from people who hadn't bothered to sit down again.

The Peabody concert was my first lesson in how to handle musical pressure; and if you don't count all the water that flowed from my eyes and nose to my sleeve, I handled it well. However, I had a second lesson a few weeks later, just before turning ten, and this time I earned an unconditional F.

Although I was still only nine, I played the organ well enough for Sister Serena to give me a new Bach piece to play at the following Sunday service. I was proud to be the youngest organist at Our Lady of Lourdes, where I played for novena on Monday afternoons; but when I began to practice the new piece, I was dismayed to discover that I would need more than a week to learn it, perhaps a year or two. At least I knew I wouldn't be using the wrong pedals because I couldn't reach any of them.

All week, I struggled desperately to learn the piece, which was much harder than the pieces I had learned from Bach's *Anna Magdalena Notebook*. This one was much harder than those that Bach had written for his young daughter. My playing it the following Sunday would be the day the music died.

By Friday morning, I was in a panic, dreaming of a Stuka dive-bombing the organ. Then, in a burst of criminal splendor, it came to me: I would simply unplug the organ so it would seem to be broken! And so, late Friday afternoon, I sneaked through the empty church with the determination of

Quasimodo and pulled out the organ plug, which was in a different room from the instrument.

In shutting down the organ, I also was shutting down my guaranteed humiliation. I was certain my sabotage wouldn't be detected: Because the plug was so far from the organ, people would be mystified by its malfunction. A perfect crime, the way a critic might have described my playing of that piece.

And then, I went to Sister Veronica with the unfortunate news.

"Sister, the organ got broken," I told her. "I don't know what happened to it."

"Haven't you been playing it all week, Charles?" she said.

"Yes, Sister, all week until now. It must've run out of . . . out of . . . organ stuff."

"*Organ* stuff? Let us take a look at it."

As if accompanying my executioner, I walked to the organ with Sister Veronica, who needed no more than ten seconds to follow the cord to the other room, where she said, "Why, someone *unplugged* it. Imagine that!"

Not much imagining was needed by one of us.

"It looks like that's why it's not working," I said, a shrewd little electrician.

"Now who could have *done* something like that?" she said.

"I wish I could help you," I said.

More than that, I wished I could help myself.

"Well, we shall certainly find out," she said. "Everyone will stay after school today until the criminal confesses."

"Criminal" seemed a bit harsh. "Dumbest kid in Baltimore" would have covered it nicely.

In silence, Sister Veronica and I walked to the office of Sister Serena. All the way, I wondered: What will she do to me if I confess? What will the boys do to me if I *don't*? What will my mother do to me if Sister Serena and the boys let me live?

When we reached Sister Serena, Sister Veronica said, "Sister, somebody unplugged the organ."

The case did not need Sherlock Holmes to shorten the list of suspects.

"Charles," said Sister Serena, "have you any idea who might have unplugged the organ?"

I toughed it out for a couple of seconds and then said, "I think it was me."

"I think it was *I*."

Only Sister Serena could have judged your morals and grammar at the same time.

"Yes, Sister."

"And you say you *think* it was?" she said.

"I'm pretty sure it was . . . I," I said.

That didn't sound right, but neither did the organ and I had to concentrate on that.

"*Pretty* sure?" said Sister Serena.

"I did it."

"Charles, I am *shocked*! *Shocked*!"

Where had I heard those words? Of course: from Claude Rains in a terrific new movie called *Casablanca* that I was about to tell to Sue Einstein. Perhaps to give myself courage, I thought about *Casablanca* and tried to steel myself by tuning to the strains of *La Marseillaise*.

If I had already read as much poetry as I have read since that time, I could have let Keats defend me by telling Sister Serena:

Heard melodies are sweet, but those unheard
Are sweeter.

And she would have replied:

No, it is better to hear lots of sound,
Which comes when you don't have the plug on the
ground.

"Charles! Do you *hear* me?" she said. "Where is your *mind*? It is such a *good* mind, but not at this moment."

"I'm sorry, Sister Serena," I said. "Please don't be shocked."

"Charles, I think it might be a good idea if you stayed after school for an hour every day next week."

It didn't seem like such a good idea to me, but this wasn't the time to make that point.

"I'm really sorry, Sister. It won't happen again."

I had given her unique contrition: a promise not to unplug the organ a second time.

"Why did you *do* it?" she said. "You play the organ so *well*."

"Other pieces, Sister, not this; I just couldn't learn it. But I'm really good with 'Like a Strong and Raging Fire'—and also 'Cheer, Cheer for Old Notre Dame.' "

"Would you rather play 'Like a Strong and Raging Fire' on Sunday? The Notre Dame song feels less appropriate."

"I certainly would!"

And so, that Sunday morning, my nimble fingers announced that strong and raging fire. Of course, I probably could have played even that one a little better. My fire might not have raged, but it clearly was annoyed.

A Stuka dive bomber

Relaxing at the age of nine

—❦—

Reading, Writing, and
Is Maine in Spain?

MY LOST CHORDS on the church organ gave me the chance to have an hour more education every day for a week. This extracurricular work, however, didn't feel like punishment because I liked school and was good at it. I could not have been called a nerd because anthropologists hadn't yet discovered that particular pen-packed species. Moreover, American schools in the forties were dominated by nerd forebears, kids who respected their teachers because they didn't know any better, kids who wore white shirts and sat silently with their hands folded on desks while listening with washed ears to things that many *college* students today feel are optional to know—for example, the location of France.

Most Americans today don't know much more about geography than how to spell it. Last summer, two married friends of mine began a drive from New York City to Portland, Maine.

"On the way there," said the wife, "why don't we stop off in Buffalo and see the Whites?"

"If we can arrange an airlift," the husband replied. "Honey, Buffalo is nowhere *near* Maine."

"Well, they're both above us, right?"

"Yes, and so is Sweden. Now I understand what happened to Amelia Earhart."

That wife, who had not spent 1942 in the fourth grade of Our Lady of Lourdes, had thought that Buffalo was northeast of New York, in the direction of Des Moines. Like so many Americans today, she had a grasp of geography that was popular on the *Santa Maria*.

A friend of mine at CBS recently told me that his daughter, a highly intelligent tenth grader, had said, "Dad, this year let's take a vacation in Bermuda. I've never been to the Caribbean."

"Neither has Bermuda," my friend had replied. "It's the same latitude as South Carolina."

"Latitude?"

"You know what that means, don't you?" her father had nervously asked.

"Getting permission for something, right?"

Geography was Greek to her, the language spoken in those islands off Spain.

How Sister Serena, Sister Veronica, Sister Mary Frances, and Sister Ursula would have shaken their cowls at the findings of the 2002 Global Geographic Literacy Survey of more than three thousand eighteen-to-twenty-four-year-old Americans:

About 80 percent of these young people could not locate Israel, Iran, or Iraq on a map. It is, of course, confusing when everything starts with an I.

The location of the Pacific Ocean was a mystery to 29 percent.

And about 11 percent of these young Americans could not locate on a map that remoteness called the United States. To all of these people, it was 1491.

Equally disturbing—no, not disturbing but beyond belief—was another survey revealing that 42 percent of the children in Texas's elementary schools could not name the country directly south of Texas. They probably did not even remember the Alamo, where Texas fought so bravely against New Mexico. The sisters at Our Lady of Lourdes might have despaired at trying to teach these so-called students and simply lit candles for them.

In the fourth grade of that little school now lost in the mists of time, I learned geography so well that I shamelessly showed off my command of it. One day when I was with Sue Einstein, I first presented to her a magnificent new film called *Yankee Doodle Dandy*, for which I not only sang "Yankee Doodle Dandy" and "Grand Old Flag," but even danced a few steps.

And then, as if she hadn't suffered enough, I said, "Betcha can't name the two cities that once were capitals of Libya at the same time."

In spite of her name, Miss Einstein looked at me as if she didn't know that Libya had even *one*.

"Why did they need *two*?" she said.

"I'm not sure," I said. "I guess it's always good to have an extra. So can you name 'em, Sue?"

"Charlie, I bet even the people in *Libya* can't name them."

"Tripoli and Benghazi," I insufferably said. "Okay, here's an easier one: Betcha think the capital of Montana is *Butte*."

And now she looked at me as if wishing that I were in Montana right then.

"Do I get a prize?" she said. "Like *The Sixty-Four-Dollar Question*?"

"No, just for fun. I love geography!"

"Me too, but not right now."

108

"Okay, here's a real easy one: Which part of Africa has the most tigers?"

"The . . . most tigers? The . . . uh . . . part that isn't *cities*, right? The *wild* part?"

"Wrong: *No* part. There are no tigers in Africa. Except maybe in the zoos."

"Why did they leave?" she said.

"They never came. They're only in Asia."

"I don't think about tigers too much. Or all the capitals of Liberia."

"Libya."

"Charlie, you know a lot of things, but some of them nobody else wants to know."

"Well, I bet you want to know *this*. You know the poem called 'The Road to Mandalay'?"

"*Everyone* knows that poem."

"Willard Wallaby doesn't. Well, here's the thing: Sister Veronica would've flunked Rudyard Kipling in geography. He says the dawn comes up like thunder out of China 'cross the bay, but the dawn *can't* come up like thunder or like *anything* out of China 'cross the bay, because Mandalay isn't *on* any bay next to China. It's on the Irrawaddy River. So Kipling *should* have said, 'And the dawn is not too shoddy/When it hits the Irrawaddy.' "

"Hey, Charlie, that's *good*."

"You really think so? I just wrote it."

"Maybe you'll be a poet when you grow up."

"I want to be in radio. There are no poems on the radio."

"*Sure* there are," said Sue. " 'Don't despair, use your head, save your hair, use Fitch Shampoo.' "

"That's a song and it doesn't rhyme very much. Want to hear another one I just wrote?"

"Oh, yes."

The moment for Lord Byron had come.

"Okay, here it is: Roses are red, violets are blue, all other flowers have colors too."

For a moment, Sue was speechless, like the first audience at Stravinsky's "Rites of Spring." At least I was spared the vegetables the Stravinsky audience threw, perhaps because Sue was carrying none.

"That's . . . that's . . . really . . ." she began, searching for an adjective that perhaps didn't exist. "*Something*," she finally said.

She might have called it nothing, but something was more accurate because something it certainly was: a poem that might have been written by the most literate of the Three Stooges.

Now that my poetry had disarmed her, now that I had her as off balance as my own mind, I wondered if *this* was the moment to ask Sue to be my girl. And so, with the courage of Lou Gehrig, but feeling more like Lou Costello, I said, "Sue . . . Sue, I was wondering . . ."

That was half of it, the easier half.

After a few seconds of silence, she said, "Yes?"

"I was wondering if . . ."

Adding one word was moving in the right direction. In another few minutes, I might even arrive.

". . . if you would be . . . if you would like to be . . . if you would mind being . . ."

And that was it. I could say no more; I would have to finish the sentence in three or four years.

"Being what, Charlie?"

"In the Felix Mackiewicz Fan Club."

"Sure," she said. "Who *is* he?"

"The Polish DiMaggio."

"Who's DiMaggio?"

My noble efforts to brighten Sue Einstein's childhood with performances of poems that sounded like bad translations from the Chinese were less successful than my cinematic standup for her. In fact, I was defeated only by a film called *Steamboat Willie*, Walt Disney's first Mickey Mouse cartoon, which Mary Ann and I saw several times in our basement with an eight-millimeter projector. I could not

111

have dazzled Sue with *Steamboat Willie* because re-creating a silent film was a challenge beyond even my awesome talent for turning art into something annoying. Why didn't I bring Sue to my basement to see *Steamboat Willie*? Because it was 1942; and a boy just didn't bring a girl to his basement in 1942, unless he wanted her to lend him a sump pump.

And so, with *Steamboat Willie*, I had to settle for entertaining only Mary Ann, although she may not have considered it that. Made in 1928, *Steamboat Willie* had musical sound in theaters, but was silent in my basement—silent, that was, except for the enrichment of my mouth. In the film, Willie makes music by playing certain animal parts, such as a cow's udder, and I felt moved to give Mary Ann what she was missing in a print with no sound. Every time Mickey played the cow, I used my formidable mouth to make music that resembled a cross between a harmonica and someone having gum surgery. On the real sound track, Mickey played "Turkey in the Straw." Mary Ann, however, had a turkey of another kind.

"Charlie, are you sick?" she said.

"I feel great!" I said.

"Then why are you moaning?"

"That's the music for Mickey . . . Okay, here it comes again: He's playing the cow!"

And now my mouth aspired for "Oh Susannah," but instead produced a sound that brought to mind a small menagerie.

"*That's* not playing a cow," said Mary Ann.

"Oh yeah?" I said. "You ever heard one played?"

"But Charlie, cows don't make 'Oh Susannah.'"

"In the South they do."

~

All that year, I had a crush on Sue Einstein, but I had to woo her only with my mind: My body wasn't wooing material, because Sue was taller than I. So many of the girls in school were taller than the boys that I used to wonder: Was a short man allowed to marry a tall woman? And then I was elated by a newsreel about the marriage of the most popular movie star of 1942, Mickey Rooney, and a stunningly beautiful new star named Ava Gardner, who looked down on Mickey from above.

I didn't play the game of guessing movie stars' names from their initials with Sue because most of her movies came secondhand through me and I didn't want her to miss them all and feel stupid. That game I saved for Mary Ann, who had no trouble guessing Mickey Rooney when I asked her, "Who's M. R.?" I stumped her, however, with, "Who's A. G.?"

"Arthur Godfrey," she said.

"Wrong!" I said. "Ava Gardner! Arthur Godfrey is just on the radio."

Just on the radio. There was no *just* in my dream, and Arthur Godfrey happened to be my idol. His show came from nearby Washington, and I used to imitate him when I was alone in my room.

"How *ah* ya, how *ah* ya, how *ah* ya?" I would say before singing "Seems Like Old Times."

My only problem in being the next Arthur Godfrey was that Godfrey played the ukulele and I played the organ. The ukulele was better: It never made you think that someone had just died.

James Cagney in *Yankee Doodle Dandy*

A Catholic school classroom very much like my own

—🖋—

Above the Orioles, My Bluebird

IN 1942, WHEN AMERICAN children knew both their place and their location, Mary Ann and I happily walked a half mile every day to learn such obscure things as the whereabouts of the Pacific Ocean. Our Lady of Lourdes was a small parish school in which all eight grades were taught by four nuns. You don't need a lofty IQ to figure out that four nuns could not have taught eight grades unless the grades were combined in twos: When I was in the fourth grade, we had third graders too, but I suffered them with grace.

Those four nuns were members of the Sisters of Charity of St. Vincent de Paul, an order that took vows of poverty, chastity, and obedience. I was still too young to realize that such a vow was considerably more than the Pledge of Allegiance.

⌣

Because we loved geography, Mary Ann and I broadened the initials game to include places on the map.

"What's A. G.?" I asked her one day.

"You can't use movie stars *or* radio stars for *places*," she said.

"This *is* a place."

"I'll tell you tomorrow."

"Oh no, the rules are you gotta answer the same day."

"Okay, it's . . . it's . . . the Atlantic Gulf."

"Atlantic *Gulf*? That's a *gasoline*. There's no such place."

"Okay then . . . it's . . . it's the . . . African Gelt."

"The African *Gelt*? You made that up too."

"I mean the place in the middle that has all that grass. The *grassy* place."

"Oh, you mean *veldt*."

"Right!"

"That's not an official place."

"Okay, Charlie, I give up."

"American Guam!"

"*What*? It's not called *American* Guam. It's nobody *else's* Guam. I mean, that's like saying American Baltimore."

"Okay, what's M. R.?"

"You're not thinking of another movie now."

"No, no, a *place*. A *big* place."

"I . . . it . . . I give up."

"Mother Russia!"

Mother Russia was no more formidable than ours. Every night after Mary Ann and I had finally done our homework, our mother checked it and even gave us quizzes, which covered all the subjects we had been studying: geography, arithmetic, history, English, science, and spelling. And her educational aids were memorable: From time to time, she got my attention by throwing a book at me.

I remember the first time she underscored her correction with this audiovisual aid. My English assignment that night had been to parse ten sentences. I do not mean to insult younger readers by explaining what parsing a sentence is, but I suspect that these days more sentences are commuted than parsed. Parsing means identifying all the sentence's parts of speech, such as its nouns, verbs, adjectives, adverbs, and prepositions. It is, of course, hard to parse the speech of many young people today because every fourth word they say is "like," and the grammarians at the University of Chicago are still trying to figure out what that "like" is.

And so, that evening, my mother picked up my English book and said, "What is the subject and what is the predicate in this sentence: 'The boy stood on the burning deck.'"

"Well, the subject is English," I replied and a second later the book arrived at my chest. It was the first time I had seen that literature could take flight. I envied that boy who was merely on a burning deck.

"Are you trying to be *funny?*" my mother cried. "Because learning English has never been very funny to me. When you grow up, do you want to conduct orchestras or trolleys?"

"Oh, you mean the *other* subject," I quickly said. "Sorry, Mom; it's the *boy*—or else the *burning deck*. Definitely one of those."

"You've been listening to the *radio* instead of studying," she said. "You've been listening to all that junk!"

"Mom, the radio isn't junk. *The Quiz Kids—The Quiz Kids* teach me things!"

"And you think they got to be quiz kids by *listening* to *The Quiz Kids?*"

She asked me this question sixty-one years ago and I'm still trying to think of the answer.

⌐

That boy foolishly standing on the burning deck was from one of the poems I loved to memorize. Our Lady of Lourdes gave us extra credit for memorizing poems, but I would have remembered them for nothing. At the age of nine I was already being moved by such music as "Let me live in a house by the side of the road and be a friend to man" and "Abou Ben Adam, may his tribe increase." What a blessedly pre-PC time that was, for today a schoolboy in that roadside house would be told not to befriend any stranger, and the stranger, no matter how weird, would be a *person*, not a man. And Abou Ben Adam might be told to consider birth control.

My love for poetry also inspired me to continue writing some of my own, to do ever better than "All other flowers have colors too," a challenge that wouldn't be a daunting one. Leaving my flora period, I moved into fauna with the lyrical zoology of something called "The Bluebird of Happiness." It is your good fortune that I cannot remember a line of it, although the writer of the song whose title I stole may still remember it. I do cringe to remember that I recited it to a girl in my class named Rosemary Ruddy, who had long blonde hair and a smile that could light up a room, if it was a small one.

With Rosemary, I was oratorically unfaithful to Sue Einstein. Rosemary was luckier than Sue, because "The Bluebird of Happiness" was considerably shorter than my synopsis of any film.

She was my safety love: If, in the next ten or fifteen years, I found the courage to ask Sue to be my girl and she

121

merely laughed for about a minute, I would put the same question to Rosemary, and perhaps also line up new bench strength.

⌒

Yes, at nine I was more in love with language and the sound of it in my voice than I was with either Rosemary or Sue, who were hearing the first forgettable presentations of *The Osgood File.* I also loved the sound of my voice in debates at the school, where the sisters trained us to be able to argue either side of any issue with the disingenuousness of politicians.

Before one debate called "Victory Gardens: Good or Bad," Sister Ursula said to me, "Charles, I want you to take the con."

Take the con! For a moment, I had a vision of glory, my taking command of a destroyer in the war I was helping to fight; but then I sensed that Sister Ursula had meant something else.

"Take the . . . con?" I said, reluctantly leaving the Navy. "How do you do that?"

With a smile, she replied, "It means against. In the debate on victory gardens, I want you to say why they are bad. That's the harder side, of course, but you're a very bright boy."

Of course I was. No *stupid* boy would have unplugged

an organ, run away from home, supplemented his diet with crayons, or put a piece of the morning news in his ear.

That day after school, while refreshing my mind by listening to eight radio serials, I thought about my almost impossible case in the debate. Could even Mister District Attorney have said why victory gardens were bad? How could *any* garden have been bad? It would have been easier to attack Eleanor Roosevelt. It would have been easier to say that "Stop Beatin' 'Round the Mulberry Bush" was not great music.

The following day at school, I made what may have been the first attack on victory gardens in American history.

"They can give you poison ivy, poison oak, and poison sumac," I said with an ignorance of botany that was majestic: poison oaks would have been harder to find in Baltimore than Yankee fans. "Also, things can come and live there, bad things like lots of locusts." A Biblical plague seemed fitting for Our Lady of Lourdes. "And there could be skunks and snakes and bears." My ignorance now had taken a sublime leap to zoology: The last bear seen in Baltimore was a Newark Bear at the Stadium.

In spite of my bizarre imagination and my golden tongue, I lost that debate because Frank Caratini somehow was able to find reasons why victory gardens were good.

123

Those debates were the kind of mental discipline that seems to have almost disappeared from the American grammar school, where the teachers are tenderly concerned with whether their students *feel* good. In a forties grammar school, as long as you didn't have scurvy, the way you felt was considerably less important than the way you thought. No mother ever said to a teacher, "You'll have to make an allowance for Lori throwing that lunchbox at you. Her Prozac isn't blending well with her lithium right now and she's been a bit more bipolar than usual this week."

124

In my school, bipolar described only the earth, and we who were in one of its fourth grades had to know that Peary discovered the North Pole and Amundsen discovered the other, which even the most slaphappy kid knew was the South.

And no mother ever said to a teacher, "Please overlook Charles never doing any homework, removing his pants, and setting a fire or two. But he *does* feel good about everything, so please don't subject him to the pressure that calling the police sometimes brings."

Yes, when I went to school, I did feel good about everything: baseball, movies, music, radio, poetry, and also prose. Nineteen forty-two was the year that my grandfather, a man

I called Popeye, gave me a copy of *Tom Sawyer* that triggered in me the same feeling for books that Stephen Foster had triggered for music.

Instead of singing Foster, I now saw myself having even greater adventures than running away to a Baltimore theater. Like Tom, I saw myself as a pirate, a challenging role for an altar boy, but I could do it. I would have to fly the Jolly Roger on some really fast fishing boat and then fight my way aboard enemy ships in Chesapeake Bay. And steal what? Clams? And who would be my enemy? I *liked* everyone. Yes, a challenge it would certainly be.

125

⌐

One morning at school, I said to Willard Wallaby, "I just read the most terrific book: *Tom Sawyer*."

"I'll see if Classics has it," he replied.

"My grandfather said it *is* a classic."

"I mean Classic Comics," said Willard. "I just read a great one: *The Hunchback of Notre Dame*."

"They let a hunchback play for Notre Dame?"

"No, this is the *other* one, the one that's got no team. A guy who don't have great posture works in a church, see, and he falls in love with a girl, but she's already in love with either a guy or a goat, I don't remember."

Willard was referring to the first grand dumbing down

of America: a new series of comic books that made the classics digestible for people who preferred their literature in twenty-five pages of pictures.

"*I* work in a church," I said, "but we don't have any goats."

"Don't matter; you gotta read this. By Hugo somebody. What a writer! The whole thing takes ten minutes and then you can trade it for a *Captain Marvel*."

"*Tom Sawyer* took me a week."

"You trade it for anything?"

126

Mental discipline was developed in my school not just by debating or reading books without pictures, but also by learning penmanship, a skill that kids today use when they are signing for rebates on Palm Pilots. In the forties, your *hand* was your pilot as it guided a pen full of ink in the graceful loops of the Palmer method of cursive writing. To prepare our hands to do such cursive writing, we had to make row after row of neatly connected loops, mental discipline that worked for some of us while others remained loopy in spite of the loops.

Willard Wallaby, for example, was never able to take his mind out of neutral. Because the capital Q in Palmer looked like a 2, Willard one day in class was moved to say to me, "Charlie, what's the difference between a Q and a two?"

"You can't start a sentence with a two," I incisively replied.

"*Sure* you can," he said. "Too bad lacrosse is such a dumb game."

"That's the *other* too, Willard. You can't start it with the *number* two."

"*Sure* you can: Two is the number of the war."

"But you wouldn't . . . but you'd write it . . ."

I had understood the difference before Willard had begun speaking with an IQ that should have been written I2 because twelve was most of it.

"What I mean is," I said, "if a word *starts* with a number two, then you know it's a *capital* Q. I think."

"But using a number still don't make sense," he said, and suddenly I saw the Zen-like nature of his point. If the great ocean liner QE2 had been written Palmer style, it would have looked like 2E2, a name more fitting for a tug.

⌒

My mother understood the Palmer method because she understood everything; and though she sometimes reinforced my learning with UFOs—Unanswered Flying Objects—she devoted much more time to non-belligerent drillings, and not just in our home at night. On warm spring and fall afternoons, she drilled Mary Ann and me in spelling, arithmetic, and geography while we sat in the greenery of nearby Hanlon Park, in the kind of setting where Shakespeare said life presents "tongues in trees, books in the running brooks, sermons in stones, and good in everything."

There were no running brooks in Hanlon Park, just running kids; no tongues in trees, just signs on them saying LEASH YOUR DOG. And yet, our mother instinctively felt that nature was the ideal classroom. There may not have been good in everything, because here and there derelicts were asleep, but those times of alfresco learning were some of the sweetest I remember. Today, whenever I stroll through a park, I ask myself such things as how to spell *pneumonia*, what the capital of Lithuania is, and that fourth *ocean . . .*

"All right, Charles," said my mother one day in her alfresco academy, "name all the oceans."

"The Atlantic, the Pacific, the Indian," I said. "And . . . and . . ."

Suddenly distracted from the water by the land, I turned to watch a butterfly light on a juniper bush.

"Arctic!" said Mary Ann.

"She didn't ask *you*," I said.

"She wants the answer before dark."

"It's so pretty out here," I told my mother.

"It certainly is," she said. "But you can't use that as an excuse for failing the geography test."

But I wondered: It *would* have a nice ring: *Sister Serena, I couldn't get to the Arctic because Baltimore beauty got in my way.*

⌒

My greatest single moment outdoors in that very good year came on the autumn day when I went behind the house to water my sub-victory garden and suddenly discovered three little green shoots! What *were* they? Could I *eat* them? The answer didn't matter: There was no need to analyze a miracle. If they were poisonous, I'd try to get them to the Germans; but if they were any form of strawberries, watermelons, or papayas, I would have produced a small but splendid message that there was hope to win the war, that no one should ever underestimate Americans, especially the Luther Burbank of Edgewood Road.

129

Winston Churchill gives the "V" for Victory sign

Yankee Doodle Dandy

BY THE END of that year, the war had begun to go better for the good guys. In December, Allied fliers bombed Nazi-occupied France in the greatest daylight raid of the war; American planes made their first raid on Italy with a bombing of Naples; and Russian troops drove the Germans back at the Don.

"You sure the Don is Russian?" I asked Mary Ann one day in December while putting new flags in my wall map.

"What *else* would it be?" she said.

"The *Don*? It could be in *Pittsburgh*. I mean, how'd the Russians name a river after a guy I *know*?"

"It's not named for Don Dooley," she said.

"Yeah, I guess not."

⌒

December 1942 was what Churchill called "the end of the beginning," and Americans were starting to sing:

And they'll come marching down Fifth Avenue,
The United Nations in review,
When this lovely dream will all come true,
We'll be dancing the victory polka.

132

By the end of that autumn, American Marines were defeating the Japanese on Guadalcanal. I was proud of the Marines and proud I could spell Guadalcanal, maybe the only kid who could. *Anybody* could have handled a landing on Guam.

And in November, I went beyond just spelling to savor a moment of geographic delight: American armed forces landed in North Africa and I officially certified this second front on my wall map by pinning a tiny American flag to Tangier.

Mary Ann had been following the war with me; in fact, she had been following it ahead of me, as I learned that November day.

"Why is the new flag on Tangier?" she said.

"Didn't you see the *Sun*?" I said. "We just landed *troops* there."

"There *too?*" she said.

"Whadda ya mean *too?*"

"Well, we also landed at *Al*giers. That's really exciting: We're liberating *all of Africa*!"

"Hmmm . . ." I said, wondering just how much of Africa needed liberating.

"Maybe it's not Tangier; I better check with Dad."

At least I hadn't put the flag on Nairobi.

⌐

In mid-December, my exhilaration was cinematic again.

"Sue, I just saw the greatest movie!" I said to my best audience, the one I kept dreaming of making my girl.

"Charlie, maybe I should see this one *first*," she said, "and then you could tell it to me."

"You *could* do that," I said, "but it's sort of back-wards."

"I guess you're right," said the only American who was given a libretto to American films.

"Okay," I said, "here it is: It's called *Now, Voyager*."

"*Now, Voyager?*" she said. "What does that mean? Take a trip now instead of later?"

"It might," I said, hoping she would stop questioning a title that made no sense to me either. "It's all about ciga-rettes. Everybody keeps lighting them in different ways and one guy lights two at *once*."

"That's the *story*? How to *smoke*?"

"No, I think it's even more than that. One woman throws herself down the *stairs*."

"Why?"

"To make her daughter pay attention to her."

"And the daughter saw her roll down?"

"No, but she sure *heard* about it."

"So she paid attention after that."

"And there's lots of poetry in the picture. Bette Davis— she's the star and she's the reason that lady came downstairs headfirst—says to a guy, 'Don't ask for the moon. We have the stars.' "

"He asked her for the moon?"

"*I think* he did. *Somebody* did. I don't remember every line, Sue; I'm just giving you the ones you should know."

"How was Bette Davis supposed to give anyone the *moon*?"

I was starting to wonder if I should have switched to a revival of *Pride of the Yankees*.

"He didn't want the *real* moon," I said. "It's *poetry*."

"Yes, that's beautiful, I guess. I just read 'The Charge of the Light Brigade.' "

"That's got no moon and a poem's better with the moon. Like 'Moon over Miami.' I like to write poetry, y' know."

"You wrote 'Moon over Miami'?"

"No, somebody beat me to that one. But listen to *this* one *I* wrote:

If something is shining,
You'll know pretty soon
Whether that something's
The sun or the moon.

At this point, she might have been wishing that I would be hit by an asteroid. However, like Cyrano de Bergerac, I knew how to try to conquer a young woman only with words. I couldn't do it with a sword or even an oyster pick—my days as Baltimore's Zorro were over—and playing "The Happy Farmer" had a limited power to raise her pulse. But *this* at last was the moment for The Question, the one I'd been trying to find the courage to ask her all year. If I couldn't ask her after telling her about the shining moon, then she would have to be somebody *else*'s girl. And it was the awful thought of Sue drifting into Willard Wallaby's arms that finally propelled my mouth to say:

"Sue, will you be my girl?"

"Why not?" she replied.

They were not exactly the words of Cleopatra or Bette Davis: They were the words of Marjorie Main. But they weren't a no, and if they didn't make the angels sing, they did at least start a hum in my heart.

135

⌐

The moon shone not just in my poetry but also in what may have been the best moments of the good feeling of America in the forties, moments that filled our house with "By the Light of the Silvery Moon," "On Moonlight Bay," and "Moonlight in Vermont." If any one scene was the essence of that *gemütlich*, and the German term for warm congeniality was certainly a fitting one for Baltimore, it was the whole family gathered around the piano after dinner to sing.

136

If a family gathers around a piano after dinner today, they have gathered because the TV is there, ninety-six channels beside the eighty-eight keys; but the four Woods, like millions of other Americans in the forties, were an early-evening quartet whose sound made up in heart what it lacked in pitch. We sang less like the Von Trapps than like Harry von Zell, whose rich voice on *Burns and Allen* was close to my father's. In fact, the voice that my father raised in those quartets was precisely the one I have now; he lives in every broadcast of *The Osgood File*.

We sang in those evening musicales because we loved the songs and loved each other and loved a country that was starting to win a titanic struggle against absolute evil. And we put as much feeling into that bittersweet ballad "Pistol

Packin' Mama" as we put into "You're a Grand Old Flag";
we made "Open the Door, Richard" as deeply moving as
"Over There"; and we captured the lyrical poignancy of "Is
You Is Or Is You Ain't My Baby?" as soulfully as that of "I'll
Be Seeing You."

On long car trips to our grandparents in Massachusetts,
we also sang in the car, songs like "Row, Row, Row Your
Boat." Of course, there *is* no song like "Row, Row, Row
Your Boat," a round that ends only when one of the singers
goes mad. And when we weren't singing "Row, Row, Row
Your Boat"—I wonder how we stopped—we sometimes
counted cows. Do any kids in cars today take livestock in-
ventories? By doing all their counting on tiny glowing
screens, they are missing something, though I'm not sure
what it is.

137

At the end of the year, I began to hear the songs from
Yankee Doodle Dandy and they were as intoxicating to me
as the songs of Stephen Foster. They quickly became my fa-
vorites at the Wood Family Follies. In fact, I even wrote a
George M. Cohan variation on "Mary" for my sister:

For it was Mary Ann, Mary Ann, long before the
fashion came.

And if there's one thing there
That's not hot air
It's her grand old name.

The end of 1942 was just one week before I turned ten. In New York City, a gaunt young singer named Frank Sinatra was about to light up the lives of thousands of young women at the Paramount Theater. Although I was pretty good with words and music myself, I was still an innocent child. I think, however, that I always must have sensed how happy I had been through all the days of that year; and with a look back now, I can put my feeling in the style of one of Sinatra's later songs:

When I was nine years old,
It was a very good year
For baseball games and movie names
And radio shows,
And pumpkins, in rows.

When I was nine years old,
It was a very good year
For Mary Ann and dark-eyed Sue
And Rosemary too,
Little loves that I knew.

When I was nine years old
It was a very good year
For Hanlon fun and tossing The Sun
And rounding those hands
On baby grands.

But time moves faster now and when I go back
The places are all
So dreamlike and small.
But through time's sweet haze
I can still see the days
They are shining and clear—
In that very good year.

139

PHOTO CREDITS